Henry Hamilton Maxwell

Memoir on swords, etc

Henry Hamilton Maxwell

Memoir on swords, etc

ISBN/EAN: 9783741170751

Manufactured in Europe, USA, Canada, Australia, Japa

Cover: Foto ©Thomas Meinert / pixelio.de

Manufactured and distributed by brebook publishing software
(www.brebook.com)

Henry Hamilton Maxwell

Memoir on swords, etc

Vol. 131.   Price 1s.

MEMOIR ON SWORDS.

By COLONEL MAREY.

With Illustrations.

TRANSLATED FROM THE FRENCH BY

LIEUT.-COL. HENRY HAMILTON MAXWELL,
Bengal Artillery.

LONDON:—JOHN WEALE.

MEMOIR ON SWORDS,

ETC.

BY

COLONEL MAREY,

COMMANDING THE 1ST REGIMENT OF CUIRASSIERS.

TRANSLATED FROM THE FRENCH

BY

CAPT. & LIEUT.-COL. HENRY HAMILTON MAXWELL,

BENGAL ARTILLERY.

TO WHICH ARE ADDED

NOTES AND ENGRAVINGS.

ALSO

TRANSLATOR OF CAPTN. TAUBERT'S WORK ON THE USE OF FIELD
ARTILLERY ON SERVICE, FROM THE GERMAN, BEING
VOL. 115 IN THE SERIES.

LONDON:

JOHN WEALE, 59, HIGH HOLBORN.

1860.

LONDON:
BRADBURY AND EVANS, PRINTERS, WHITEFRIARS.

CONTENTS.

LIST AND EXPLANATION OF THE PLATES.

Fig. 1.—To illustrate the form of the Turkish sword-hilt. This sabre is copied from specimen No. 845, U. S. Museum, Whitehall, and has the following legend attached to it:—"Damascus Sabre, given by Yusuf Karaman Ali, Pasha of Tripoli, to Captain W. H. Smyth, R.N., K.F.M." It is flame-shaped, as recommended by the author for ships' cutlasses, or other blades which are not worn in scabbards. This flamboyant shape was common enough in the old straight long double-handed swords of the chivalric era.

Fig. 2.—British Old Pattern Light Cavalry Sword ; the old point of which has been cut off to bring the new point nearer to the line of impulse, and thus to improve its thrusting capabilities.

Fig. 2 b.—British New Pattern Light Cavalry Sword.

Fig. 2 c.—New Hilt as applied to the blade of the above. There is strictly no "tang" to this sword ; but the blade is prolonged to the length of the hilt. Two pieces of solid leather are then riveted, one on each side, of the prolongation of the blade, which is visible at the back and front. This arrangement has the important advantage of strengthening the attachment of the blade and hilt. The old method was subject to the inconvenience of the sword-tang getting loose in the grip, and not unfrequently the sword broke off at the tang, in giving a powerful blow.

Fig. 3.—Illustrates the action of cutting, and the manner in which a sliding cut backwards or forwards has the same effect as though the blade were infinitely sharper than it actually is. (Borrowed from Piobert).

Fig. 4.—Illustrates the effect of wounds made with sabres of various degrees of curvature, and the high ratio of increase as the angle of curvature increases.

Fig. 5.—Illustrates the mechanical effect of a blow as regards the different parts of a sword.

Fig. 6.—Ditto ditto.

Fig. 7.—Illustrates the recommendation of the author that the thickness of the metal of swords intended for striking should be greatest, not at the back as is usually the case, but at the middle, or at two-thirds of the breadth measured from the edge. This blade, however, is thickest still nearer the edge, being at about one-third of the breadth therefrom. This figure is a copy of a sketch I made in Turkey, of a sword the property of an officer in the Ottoman service. The weapon was made at Baghdad. The steel was of the quality termed "Tabau," and its peculiar shape is called "Bala," an appellation it may have got from its great power of cut, or, technically, percussive force ; the word "bala," in Arabic, meaning "vengeance." It was valued by its owner at 7000 piastres, or about 55*l.* to 58*l.*

Figs. 8, 9 *a*, 9 *b*, 10, and 11.—Sections of various forms of swords, varied so as to stiffen the blade.

Figs. 12 to 20, both inclusive, illustrate the mechanical effect of the point.

Figs. 21 to 25, both inclusive, illustrate the nature of wound made in giving the curved point.

Figs. 26 to 32, both inclusive, illustrate the nature of wound, as well as the forces developed, in giving the straight-point.

In both these sets of illustrations, the light shading shows the body wounded, and the dark shading the shape of the wound itself.

Fig. 33.—Shows the form of the wound made by a blade moving onwards in a plane, and at the same time revolving in the same plane round the heel of the hilt. The above remark as to shading applies to this figure likewise.

Fig. 34.—Illustrates the blade having the edges at its concavity. This
figure is copied from a yataghan in the Tower Armoury.

Fig. 35.—Illustrates the fact, that a blade acting with an edge oblique to
the direction of the cut has the same effect as a blade whose edge is
perpendicular to it, but whose line of action is oblique at the
surface of the body struck. This figure is a copy of the axe of a
guillotine, specimen, No. 1593 of the United Service Museum collec-
tion ; the trapezoidal blade is attached to a block of wood, on the
edges of which are tenons fitting the metal grooves of the two up-
rights of the scaffold. On the top of the block of wood is a mass of
lead, to increase the momentum, fastened thereto by means of screw-
bolts which run through from below, and are tightened by the
screw-nuts at top. The dimensions given in the figure are in
English inches. The following legend is attached to it :—"The
axe of a guillotine, cut down by the late Admiral Scott, at Guadaloupe, in 1794, at the taking of the West India Islands. Fifty
Royalists had already been decapitated by it."

Fig. 36.—Illustrates the same as Fig. 34. This weapon is called the
"Khora." It is Nepaulese, and is used, I believe, for sacrifices.
Such feats as cutting a bullock's head off, or cutting a sheep
through, at one stroke, are to be done with this arm.

Fig. 37.—Is the "Khookhri," or Nepaulese knife. It is used by these
mountaineers in war, and in every other possible way, from cutting
down a huge tree to making a toothpick, or executing very creditable carving. The ridge on the handle seems to European hands
ill-devised.

Figs. 38, 39, and 41, illustrate the shapes of daggers suitable to the thrust,
with the blade nearest the thumb or nearest the little finger, or in
other words for the straight or the curved stab. They are all of
Hindoostanee manufacture, though, possibly, of Affghan origin.

Fig. 40.—Is a curious weapon, both offensive and defensive, combining a
shield with two curved daggers : the latter are mounted in stag's
horns.

Fig. 42.—Is a curiosity in the way of small-arms. It combines the
thrusting-dagger and percussion-pistol. It is of Circassian manu-

PLATE 1.

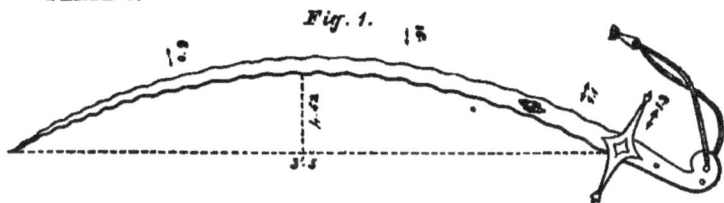

Fig. 1.

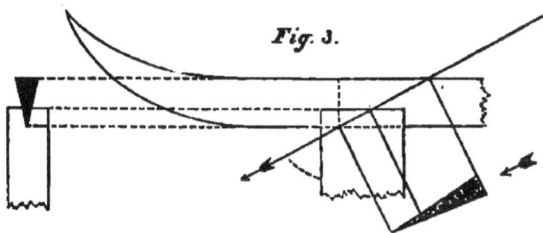

Fig. 3.

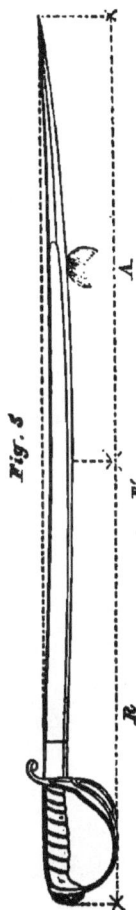

Fig. 5.

Fig. 6.

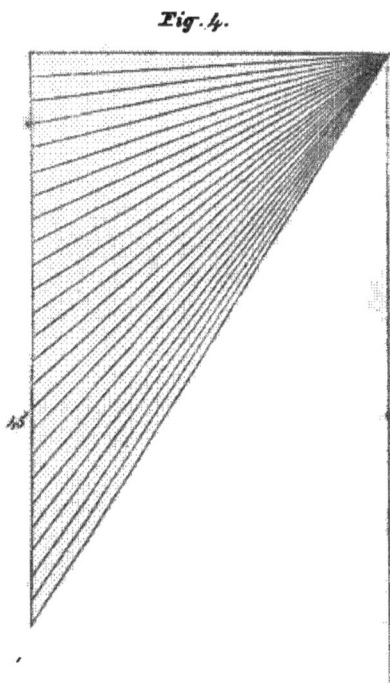

Fig. 4.

PLATE 2.

Fig. 2.

British Old Pattern Light Cavalry Sword.
Wt 2 lbs. 4 oz.

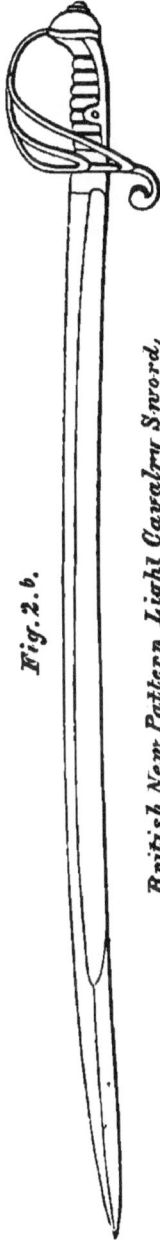

Fig. 2.b.

British New Pattern Light Cavalry Sword.
Wt. 2. lbs. 7 oz.

Fig. 2.c.

N P. Hilt

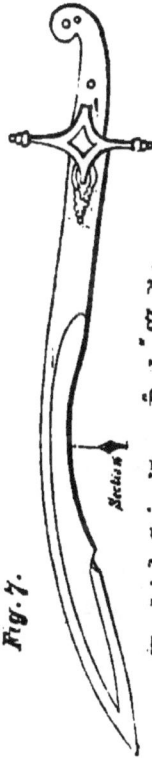

Fig. 7.

Section

Turkish Scimitar. "Bala" Shape.

PLATE 3.

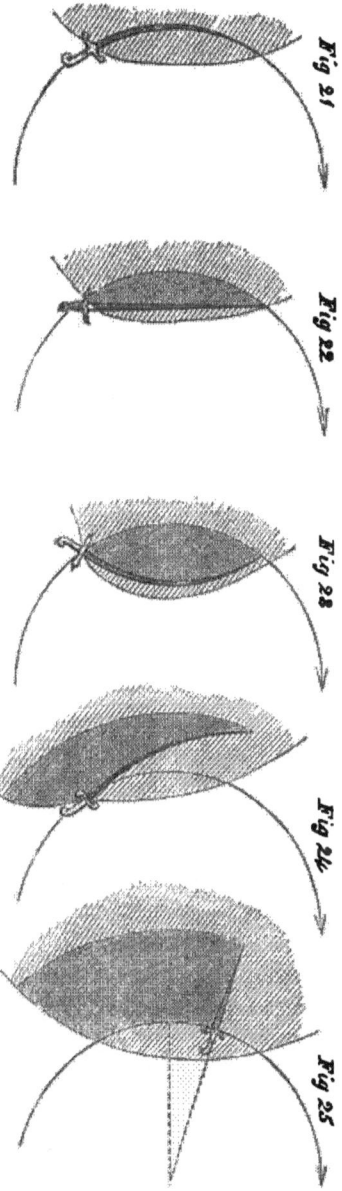

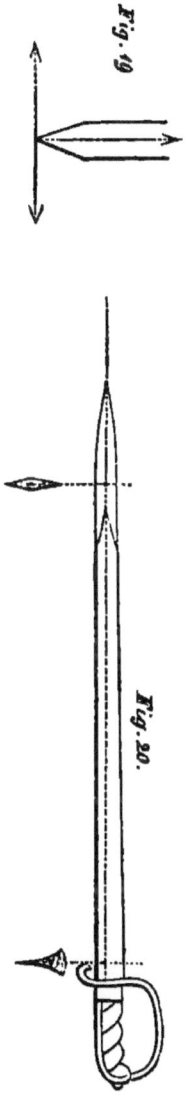

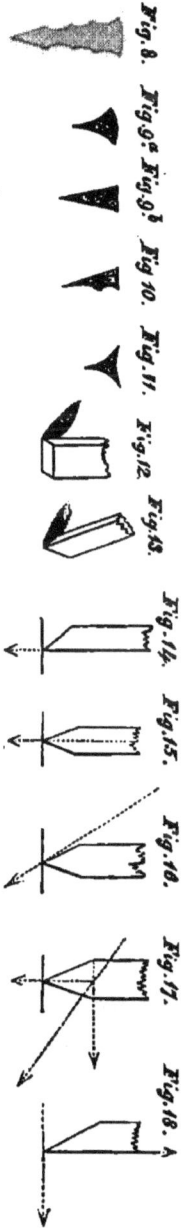

Fig. 8. Fig. 9ᵃ Fig. 9ᵇ Fig. 10. Fig. 11. Fig. 12. Fig. 13. Fig. 14. Fig. 15. Fig. 16. Fig. 17. Fig. 18.

Fig. 19.

Fig. 20.

Fig. 21

Fig. 22

Fig. 23

Fig. 24

Fig. 25

PLATE 4.

Fig. 26   Fig. 27   Fig. 28.   Fig. 29

Fig. 30.

Fig. 31.

6 in.
the Screw-bolts go through
from below.

8.25 in.
6.35 in.

9 in.

Fig. 35.

9.5 in.

15. in.

7 in.

Guillotine Axe

Fig. 32.

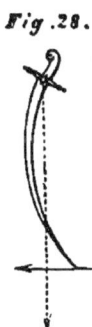

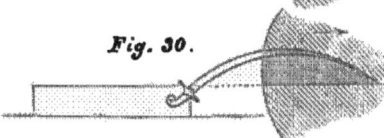

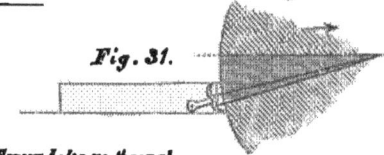

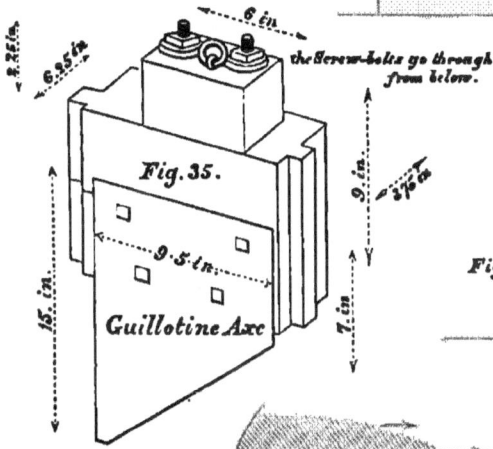

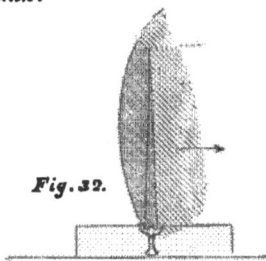

Section of Blade

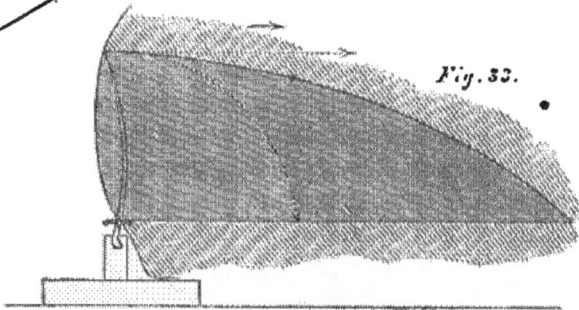

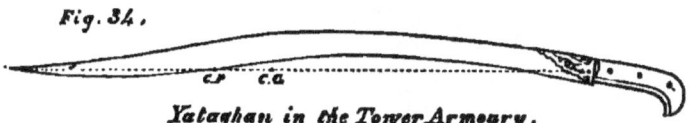

0.3

Fig. 33.

Fig. 34.

c.p   c.a

Yataghan in the Tower Armoury.

PLATE 5.

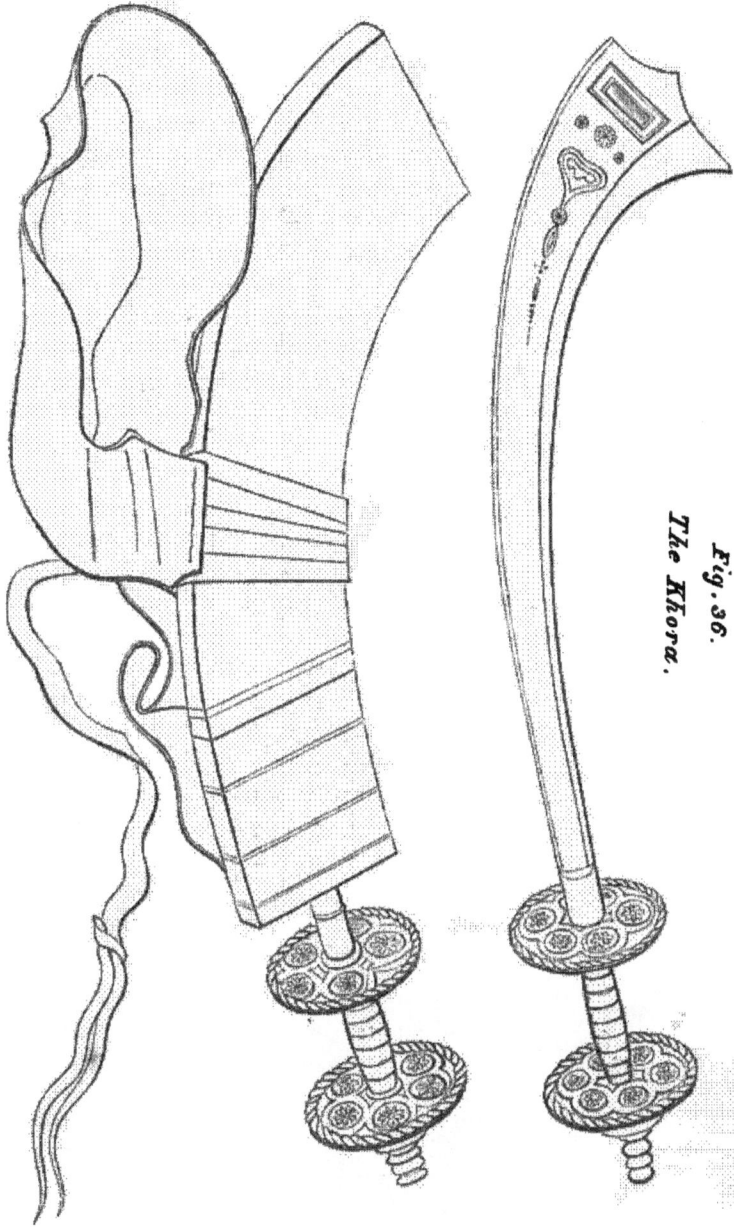

Fig. 36.
The Khora.

PLATE 6.

Fig. 37
The Koohhri.

Fig. 38.

Fig. 39.

Fig. 40.

Fig. 41.

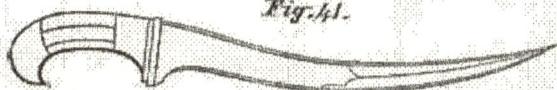

Fig. 42.

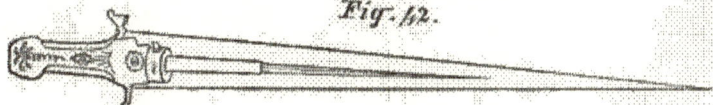

PLATE 7.

Fig. 43.

The Hindostani Tulwar.

Fig. 43 ᵃ

Fig. 43 ᵇ

Fig. 43 ᶜ

Fig. 43 ᵈ

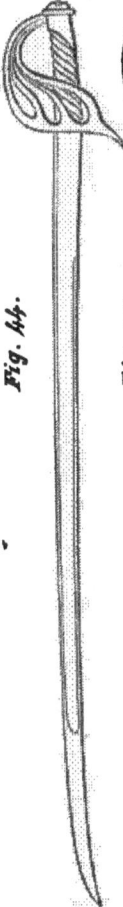

Fig. 44.

Fig. 45.

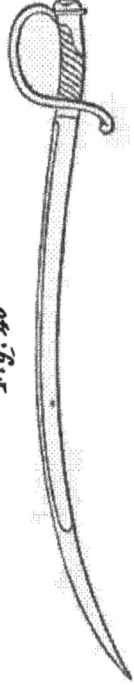

Fig. 46.

PLATE 8.

Fig. 47

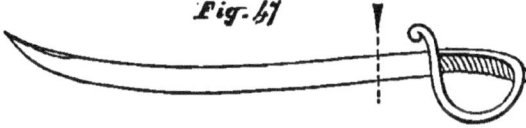

Fig. 48

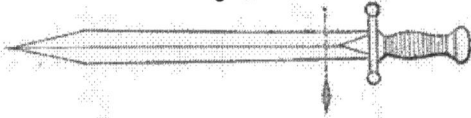

Fig. 49

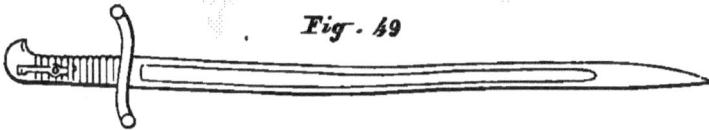

Fig. 50   1/10

Fig. 51.

m. XI

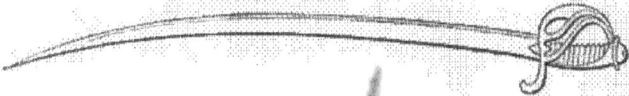

Fig. 52

m. XIII

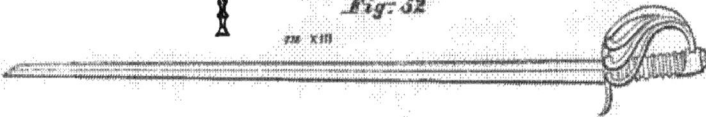

Fig. 53

m. 1816.

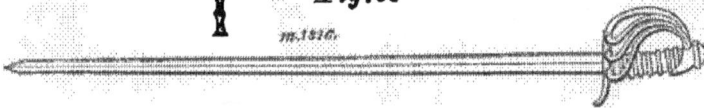

THE distinguished Officer, the Translator of the interesting "Memoir on Swords," and of the Prussian work of Capt. Taubert, in his zeal for the Military Service, seconded by the publisher, put forth a proposition for the issue of a Military Series; but which, up to the present time, has not in high places been responded to.—J. W.

RUDIMENTARY MILITARY SERIES.

WITH a vast military force in England and in India, and with all the elements of military greatness, we are undoubtedly deficient in that higher professional knowledge, without which true military vitality cannot effectually be maintained. In order to make this knowledge more accessible to the soldier and to the public at large, it is proposed to put forth in Volumes, a Series at 1s. and 1s. 6d., on such terms as will be suitable to those of limited pay.

The present volumes are faithful and careful translations from the German, by Lieut.-Col. Henry Hamilton Maxwell, of an important Prussian work on the management and service of artillery, and of a useful and interesting French work on Swords, both which I am, through the liberality of Lieut.-Col. Maxwell, enabled to issue at the price of 1s. 6d. and 1s.

The Government of the country are called upon to render their aid, by permitting the republication at a cheaper rate of the several works issued under their sanction, which are now published at a price beyond the means of those who are filling the lower grades of the army.

Military men of knowledge and experience are also solicited to contribute to this series such as would be of practical advantage to the soldier in his professional education.

Suggestions would be thankfully received by the publisher.

LIST OF WORKS PROPOSED FOR THE RUDIMENTARY MILITARY SERIES.

1. ARTILLERY.—On the Use of Field Artillery on Service.
2.   „   Laboratory Course—Manufacture of Gunpowder, and Purification of its Ingredients—Throwing up Batteries—Service of Artillery in Batteries—Service of Coast Artillery Repository Exercise.
3. CAVALRY.
4. INFANTRY—to include Musketry.
5. THE THREE ARMS.
6. COURSE OF MILITARY TOPOGRAPHY AND RECONNAISSANCES.
7. COURSE OF MILITARY ADMINISTRATION—including every detail as to Baking Bread, Fattening and Slaughtering Cattle. Rations, various in different climates, during prevalence of certain epidemics —Sanitary Measures, &c. &c.—Transport, Tents, &c.
8. FIELD FORTIFICATION—to include Siege Duties for all Arms.
9. OUTPOST DUTIES.—Advance of Rear Guards, including Treatment of Spies, both those of the enemy and own. Signals, day and night—Telegraphs, &c.
10. COMPLETE COURSE OF STUDY FOR REGIMENTAL SCHOOLS.
11. THE HORSE, AS A MILITARY ANIMAL—to include Management— Veterinary directions—Qualities—Judgment of—the Kind adapted to Draught—Riding—Burden. Likewise Camels, Bullocks, Mules, Elephants.
12. PRACTICAL GYMNASTICS.
13. INTERIOR ECONOMY OF A TROOP OR COMPANY.—Returns—Forms— Public Correspondence—Finance—Promotion—Discipline—Instruction, mental and physical—Idem of a Battalion—Embarcation— Foreign Service—Hints for the Line of March—Feet—Boots—Kit, method of carrying—Cooking in the Field and in Quarters—Water —Battle—Pitching Tents—Making Huts—Clothing—Clothing, hot and cold Climate.
14. MILITARY HISTORY AND ART.—Narratives of Battles—Why they were lost or gained—Tactics.
15. MILITARY BRIDGES—in all parts of the world.

TRANSLATOR'S PREFACE.

THE original work, of which I offer a translation to the public, was published at Strasburg in 1841, and has since become very scarce, being now out of print. It was only after repeated efforts, during several years, that I succeeded in procuring the copy I now possess, and it is a second-hand one, having been presented, as appears by an inscription in the handwriting of the author, to a friend. This copy, however, was not destined to remain quietly in my possession, as it fell into the hands of the Rohilcund mutineers, who, not understanding French, I presume, flung it out on the Grand Trunk Road, near Allyghur. Fortunately for me, it was taken to the magistrate of the district, and by means of an advertisement in a newspaper, it once more came into my possession, and I was thus enabled to make this translation.

It may be said to be "a heavy blow and great discouragement" to a man, who has resolved to translate a book, to be met at the outset by an obstacle in the

shape of the very first words of the title-page—to find
that the languages into which it is to be rendered
does not contain words capable of succinctly giving
the meaning of those in the original. Such is the case
with the work in question; and, strange to say, this is
not the first time I have met with this rebuff in a precisely similar manner. The title in the original is
"*Mémoire sur les Armes-blanches.*" The last two
words, connected by a hyphen, form a generic term, of
which we have no synonym: it includes *all portable
arms, other than fire-arms, defensive and offensive,
made of steel or iron;* thus comprising swords of all
sorts, bayonets, daggers, boarding-axes, pikes, lances,
&c., among offensive arms; and cuirasses of the heavy
dragoon and sapper, as well as helmets of all natures,
&c., among defensive. What the French term indi-
cates in two words, I have been compelled to translate
by fifteen. Any person, then, I conceive, who would
invent a word, or combination of words, and cause it
to be accepted by the military world, which would
succinctly convey the meaning of this French technical term, would make a most acceptable addition
to our essentially poor military terminology. I have
endeavoured to do so, and have failed signally, as have
many abler men to my knowledge. And lest any one
should consider the addition of such a term to our
military technical vocabulary a species of sacrilege on
our language, let me quote the words of an excellent

authority on the subject.* Alluding to the introduction of new words into the English language, he says :—" I do not refer here to purely scientific terms ; these, so long as they continue such, and do not pass beyond the threshold of the science, or sciences, for the use of which they were invented, being never heard on the lips, or employed in the writings, of any but culti- vators of these sciences, have no right to be properly called words at all. They are a kind of short-hand of the science, or algebraic notation ; and will not find a place in a rightly-constituted dictionary of the language, but rather in a technical dictionary apart by themselves." The new word, or combination of words, if even it be invented, to quote further from the same authority, should be formed " according to the analogy of formations which, in seemingly parallel cases, have been already allowed." As a further proof of the legitimacy of thus making a new word current, I may state that the Germans have literally translated " Armes-blanches " into " Blanken-waffen," and this term has been universally adopted by their military writers.

I have been induced to make and publish this translation, because I am not aware of the existence of any work on swords, &c., in the English language,

---

* The Very Reverend R. Chenevix Trench, Dean of Westminster, author of "English, Past and Present," and other admirable works on our languages, at p. 68 of the book quoted.

save a diminutive pamphlet by Wilkinson, the sword-
cutler; and because the original, recommended in the
highest terms by Thiroux, a French writer on artillery
of the first class, appeared to me to go to the bottom
of the question with the most profound sagacity, combined with practical and scientific knowledge. That
his readers, if such this translation of the author's
work is destined to have, may endorse this opinion, is
my most sincere wish.

The original work has no plates. I have endeavoured to supply what might be thought a defect,
having made sketches, and copied plates of arms,
&c., in various parts of the world for the purpose. I
trust they may tend to elucidate the text. I have
further added a few foot-notes as occasion seemed to
require.

                                        H. H. M.

   AGRA,
      Sept. 1859.

MEMOIR ON SWORDS.

PRELIMINARY.

—◆—

CHAPTER I.

OBJECT OF THE WORK.

1. BEING garrisoned at Strasburgh as an officer of artillery, I employed myself in researches upon swords. I practised with them so as to be able to use them efficiently, and acquired sufficient dexterity in so doing. The neighbourhood of Klingenthal enabled me to make up, at my own charges, a great number of swords of different patterns, all of which I tried successively. These labours were interrupted by the expedition to Algiers, and by a sojourn of nine years in Africa. Having served in that country as a cavalry officer, I always wore a sword of the pattern I propose for adoption, and found it a serviceable weapon. This memoir gives the results to which these researches led.

2. I propose to examine the reasons which determine the shape of swords, to collect them together in

B

the form of principles, and to apply these principles
to the examination of the usual patterns; finally to
deduce therefrom a few new-pattern arms, which I
submit to the lights of the general officers of artillery
and cavalry, to the end that these essays should induce
other officers to invent patterns susceptible of adoption, if those which I propose are not approved of.
Feeling certain that my ideas will be found to be
sound and of useful application, I shall consider myself fortunate if my labours conduce towards adding
to the number of the many improvements lately introduced in the various branches of the important services
of the artillery and cavalry.

3. I am aware that the success of cavalry depends
more on the ability and courage of the men than on
the shape of their swords. It is reasonable to believe,
however, that a good weapon adds to the soldier's confidence; at any rate, it may be interesting to lay down
the principles which enable us to appreciate the qualities of any given arm; and, on the other hand, any
requisite qualities being given, to determine the shape
of the blade that shall possess them.

CHAPTER II.

THE ELEMENTS OF THE QUESTION.

1. THE object of offensive steel arms is to produce
on the animal economy of an enemy serious injury,
such as shall result in his death, or in putting him

hors de combat. The requisite depth of wound has, according to time and place, been attained by striking

First—With a *surface*, more or less extensive, such as with clubs, maces, mallets of arms.

Second—With a *line*, as with all cutting weapons: sabres, axes, scythes, &c.

Third—With a *point*, as with all arms intended to be used in thrusting: lances, poniards, bayonets.

Fourth—With arms which *penetrate*, impregnated with *poisonous* substances, as were, and are still, in use in many savage nations.

The march of progressive improvement made in steel weapons is characterised by a gradual diminution —of the mark left by the body striking on the body struck, whether the former be a *surface*, a *line*, or a *point*—of the amount of exertion required to inflict a wound of the requisite depth—of the weight of the weapons—of the muscular force necessary to wield them—and likewise by an increase of their actual efficiency.

2. Contusive weapons appertain more particularly to the barbarous ages, when the metals were but little known, and when physical force was of more account than dexterity.

Poisoned arms, likewise, are only used by savage nations but little advanced in civilisation. Their arms are made of wretched materials, such as hardwood, bones, stones, &c.; they are ignorant of the method of shaping them into the most judicious forms, and they can only thus procure the means of inflicting serious injury; to them war is generally a series of single combats, in which the combatant strikes with the desire of destroying a personal enemy, and with all the bitterness of savage irritation ; while, on the other hand, war between civilised nations is carried on by masses, and, generally speaking, with coolness. It is remarkable that no ancient nation renowned for its military successes, used poisoned weapons. Nevertheless, the army which first employed these means before the invention of gunpowder, must have created a profound moral impression upon its enemies before coming to hand-to-hand combat. Poisoned, like contusive, weapons are in keeping with a state of civilisation in which a conquered enemy is scalped or eaten.

Cutting arms were and are still much used. They have attained a degree of perfection which enables them to produce the most extraordinary, not to say incredible, effects. One portion of the cavalry in Europe is exclusively armed with weapons of this nature. In France the effect of the point is more particularly relied on.

3. In nature we find the lower orders of creation armed in a manner almost analogous to ourselves, thus :

First—The effect of the blow of a club may be compared to that inflicted by the head of a ram, the trunk of an elephant, the hoof of a horse, the fist of a man, the wings of certain birds, and the tails of a crocodile and of certain fish.

Second—The tusks of a wild boar appear to be the sole cutting arms given to animal creation ; for the fangs of other creatures tear rather than cut, and seem to be intended to penetrate first, and to hold on afterwards.

Third—The tusks of an elephant, the horn of a rhinoceros, those of a bull, the canine teeth of the carnivora—their fangs, the quills of a porcupine, the peculiar arms of the saw and sword fishes, are all intended for thrusting.

Fourth—Bees, scorpions, and venomous serpents inject poisonous matter into the wounds they inflict.

Fifth—There are some animals who fight by means of projectiles: among other creatures, the ostrich.*

The offensive arms of the animal creation resemble those employed by the first men; they are generally contusive in their nature, or they give point, or empoison. The cause of this similarity is that it is extremely difficult to supply the place of the metals by other materials possessing the qualities requisite for cutting instruments.

The tusks of the wild boar, which literally cut, do not act from the centre to the point like our sabres, but by penetration primarily and cutting subsequently; they could not be much longer without prejudice to their strength.

The commonest arms are those intended for thrusting. The carnivora, who live by making war on other animals, use their incisor teeth to kill their prey, as poniards are used in stabbing.

We shall have occasion to draw inferences from the

---

* When pursued he dashes stones at his pursuers with great violence.—Cuvier.—T.

form affected by the arms given by nature to the brute creation, applicable to our own weapons.

4. Swords seem at first to have been intended for thrusting, and at a later period for cutting, and this with moderate efficiency. We shall see that these two qualities are compatible in the same arm. We will proceed to examine separately that which constitutes each of these qualities.

PART I.

OF ARMS USED FOR CUTTING.

——•——

CHAPTER I.

DISCUSSION OF THE PRINCIPLES IN ARMS USED FOR
CUTTING.

1. In making a cut, the sword is brought down
with great velocity on the body **struck**; this velocity
is obtained by a species of **rotatory** motion, engen-
dering a centrifugal force. The velocity of rotation
acts on the body cut into; the centrifugal force is
counteracted by the resistance of the wrist, and bears
upon the little finger: in cutting with a sword, using
much force, the little finger sustains very great pressure. In the Turkish scimitar (Figs. 1 and 7) the
region of the grip, whereon the little finger bears, is
very wide; in the curved British sword (Fig. 2) it is
moderately so; and in ours, not only is this part very
narrow and its angles quite sharp, but it has occasion-
ally several most injurious ridges left thereon by way
of ornament. Further, most of our swords (Figs. 44,
45, 46) hurt the little finger, and even excoriate it, if a
cut be made with force, or if "moulinets"* be prac-

———

* If a straight stick be grasped by the thumb and index-finger at their

tised with them. *The bearing of the little finger on the grip should be wide and smooth:* this is a matter of the most essential importance.

As to the line of direction of this part of the grip, it should vary according to the nature of sword exercise in use : many swords, which are acknowledged to be well made, have the grip at this point inclined to its general run and gradually sloping into it, so that the actual bearing of the little finger is situate in the rear of the junction of these two lines ; others, again, have the bearing perpendicular to the grip. I have tried both the one and the other plan, and it seemed to me that, if the first system were preferable for light swords intended exclusively for cutting, the second is more adapted for our swords, which are tolerably heavy, and intended principally for thrusting.

2. A cut is effected by the combined motions of the upper and fore arm, the wrist, and the sword in the hand. If a series of cuts be made, in each of which one of the above-named portions of the body be used separately, while the rest are kept rigid, and if the marks successively produced by the sword be left on thin wooden planks, we shall find that the cut due to the wrist motion is the most effective ; that when the whole of the motions are made in combination, the sword lies in a direct line with the fore arm, and that it often passes that line, and finally that the motion of the sword in the hand has a most notable effect. All things being in other respects identical, the greater the

junction, and if it be whirled round and round continuously, these are " moulinets."   T.

amount of space traversed by the cutting edge in equal spaces of time, the greater will be its velocity and the more effective its action.

Hence we deduce these conclusions—

1st—The grip has all the more play the narrower it is crosswise—that is, in the direction of from back to edge of the blade, but more particularly at the points where it is held by the index and little finger, these two having the greatest effect on the lever acting inside the hand.

2nd—The grip should be smooth, so that friction may not check motion in the hand, and that no unevenness of surface may hurt it. It is more especially of great importance that nothing at the grip, nor at its side, should injure the index and little finger, as is the case in several patterns.

The grip of the Mameluke sabre (Figs. 1 and 7) is smooth, narrow in the direction of the width of the blade, and wide in a perpendicular direction thereto. The curved British sword (Fig. 2),* which, like the

---

* The author all through his work speaks of the old British Light Cavalry sword as an admirable weapon for cutting, and his judgment is remarkably confirmed by the following interesting extract from Captain Nolan's book on Cavalry :—

"When I was in India an engagement took place between a party of the Nizam's irregular horse, &c. . . . . My attention was drawn particularly to the Doctor's report of the killed and wounded, most of whom suffered by the sword, and in the column of remarks such entries as the following were numerous :—

   " 'Arm cut from the shoulder.'
   " 'Head severed.'
   " ' Both hands cut off (apparently at one blow) above the wrists, in holding up the arms to protect the head.'
   " ' Leg cut off above the knee, &c.'

    .   .   .   .

" And now fancy my astonishment !

above, is very well fashioned, has a grip which **is**
narrow at both ends and bulges out in the centre ; the
bulge exerts no injurious influence.

3rd. The thumbs should not be placed on the back
of the blade in striking with the edge, as laid down in
the French regulations; for, under such circumstances, the motion in the hand and that of the wrist
cannot have play. Among nations famed for the
extraordinary effect produced in cutting, the system of
sword-exercise is in accordance with this idea.

4th. Several other positions prescribed in the French
regulations relative to the manner of using the edge
should be modified. In the motion, *" à gauche sabrez "*
(left attack), for instance, the sword is carried to the
right in the direction of the extended arm; a cut from
this position cannot possibly be a powerful one. To
produce a serious effect with a sword in this motion,

"The sword-blades they had were chiefly old dragoon blades cast from
our service. The men had remounted them after their own fashion.
The hilt and handle, both of metal, small in the grip, rather flat, not round
like ours when the edge seldom falls true ; they all had an edge like a
razor from heel to point, were worn in wooden scabbards, a short single
sling held them to the waistbelt, from which a strap passed through the
hilt to a button in front, to keep the sword steady and prevent it flying
out of the scabbard.

"An old trooper of the Nizam's told me the old English broad blades were
in great favour with them, when remounted and kept as above described ;
but as we wore them, they were good for nothing in *their* hands.

"I said, 'How do you strike with your swords to cut off men's limbs ?"
"'Strike hard, sir !' said the old trooper.

"'Yes, of course ; but how do you teach them to use their swords in
that particular way !" (*drawing it.*)

"'We never teach them any way, sir ; a sharp sword will cut in any
one's hand.'"

Pp. 110, 111, 112, "Cavalry : its History and Tactics," by Capt.
L. E. Nolan. 2nd Edit. London : 1854.

the arm should not be extended, nor should the thumb be on the back of the grip ; while the blade, instead of being in the prolongation of the fore-arm, should be thrown backwards forty-five degrees beyond the perpendicular and lie close to the shoulder : thus the cut will not only be animated with the velocity due to the arm, but further with that caused by the wrist making the point describe three-eighths of a circle in the same period of time—this being the result of the difference between the original and the proposed positions of the **sword.**

3. The edge, to act with full effect, should have the rest of the blade included in the plane it describes ; in order that the momentum resulting from the velocity and the volume should actuate it. The breadth of the blade contributes towards keeping itself in this position ; for the air has an effect upon it analogous to that of the wind upon a weathercock, the plane **of which** adjusts itself in a direction determined by the position of its pivot and the direction of the wind.

The hilt, when its centre of gravity is not in the plane of the blade, has, on the other hand, an opposite and injurious influence in the above respect. Thus in our cavalry swords the branches of the guard are placed on one side only, while the front branch is in the centre ; they consequently tend to destroy the *aplomb* (equilibrium) of the cut, and to cause **the** blade at the moment it meets with resistance from the body struck, to turn the flat of the sword in the direction of the side branches.

Swords intended exclusively for cutting are

symmetrical, and have generally but one branch; the
Turkish sabre has no branches whatever. Swords
intended for both thrusting and cutting appear to
require a defensive hilt. It is quite possible, and it
seems desirable, that it should be made symmetrical.
In many patterns it is so; but if one side of the hand
ought to be more guarded than the other, which may
be fairly admitted—as in the ordinary position in
pointing with the wrist in tierce, it requires to be
more defended on the side exposed to the enemy than
on the opposite one—it is at least desirable to diminish
the injurious influence of the want of equilibrium,
by placing the front branch not immediately in the
centre, but on the opposite side; at the **same time**
making it stouter and heavier than the other branches.
In this manner we should apparently gain as regards
an equal distribution of the weight of metal, while at
the same time the hand would be better guarded. I
have had several hilts made up of the pattern described;
the advantages gained seem to entail no corresponding
disadvantages.

4. The sharper the edge, that is to say, the narrower
the base of the triangle by which it is formed, in
proportion to the perpendicular let fall from the apex
to the base, the greater is the faculty of penetration.

Many swords have a very fine edge; this is attended
with the disadvantage of weakness. The advantage
of combining strength with an edge which cuts as
though it were very sharp, has led to the blade being
made more or less curved.

To account for the effect thus produced, let us

imagine a blade (Fig. 3) whose cross section is triangular; that this blade strikes a body obliquely, and that the oblique mark left on the blade by the body struck is double the height of the similar mark which would be left on the blade, by striking perpendicularly, or from edge to back. In the former case the blade would have cut as though the triangle which forms the cross section of the edge had for its base, the constant quantity the thickness of the back, but a double height; or, in other words, as though the angle of the edges were sensibly half less.

In a cut made with full velocity, the blade at the moment it comes in contact with the body struck should lie in the direction of the fore-arm; it strikes in a direction nearly perpendicular to the prolongation of the origin * of the blade. The greater the inclination of the part of the edge which strikes to that line, the greater will be the length of the mark left on the blade by the wound.

In the Mameluke scimitars, this inclination amounts to forty-five degrees; the length of the mark left is generally more than double the width of the blade, and it may be quintuple when the edge is slipped across the object, as usual in producing delicate effects, such as cutting a sheet of paper suspended by a thread. Thus the Turkish blade cuts as though it were from twice to five times as sharp as it actually is.

Certain wide-bladed swords and halberts have edges

* The term " origin" of the blade or hilt is used throughout both the original and the translation in a mathematical sense ; in the same manner as in treatises on the straight line or on curves, the " origin" of the one and the other is spoken of.　　　　　　　　　　　　　T.

serrated like a saw, that is to say with many teeth,
inclined to the direction of the stroke at an angle of
forty-five degrees; this facilitates penetration like the
curvature of the Turkish blade. But this formation
of the edge being essentially weak was not, and could
not, be adapted to any but the very strongest and
stoutest blades. The same may be said of the wavy
or flame-shaped edge (Fig. 1),* which moreover is
attended with the like quality.

In the British light cavalry sword (Fig. 2), which
is less curved than the Damascus blade, this effect is
still tolerably apparent; it is nearly *nil* in our patterns
which are but slightly curved. Of this we may con-
vince ourselves by examining and comparing the marks
left on the blades by the object struck in our patterns,
in other swords of equal curvature but in the opposite
direction, and in purely straight swords. We may
account for this too by remarking, that if between two
parallel lines (Fig. 4) we draw one at right angles, and
further other lines, making small angles with the perpendicular, the differences of the lengths of the lines
comprised between the two parallels is very trifling,
while it increases vastly as the angle approaches forty-
five degrees, and much more as it exceeds that angle :
thus practice and theory agree in this matter.

It is not necessary that the cutting edge should be
inclined to the origin of the blade to produce the effect
of a more acute edge; it is merely requisite to alter

---

* As a specimen of a flame-shaped or wavy blade, I give a sketch, at
Fig. 1, of a "Damascus Sabre, given by Yussuff Karaman Ali, Pasha of
Tripoli, to Captain W. H. Smyth, R.N., K.F.M.," No. 845 of the collec-
tion of arms in the United Service Museum, Scotland Yard.   T.

the direction of the force of the blow, by causing the edges to **glide upon** the object struck by a peculiar motion of the wrist from front to rear. This is practised in the broadsword exercise, in which the combatant endeavours to keep his point opposite his adversary's body as far as possible; this is termed "sawing." A sensible effect of velocity is thus obtained, without which penetration would have perhaps been impossible. The normal velocity in this cut, which is almost tangential, is feeble; consequently the steel has but a slight effect in compressing the flesh, which merely sustains a feeble pressure in a normal direction. The edge in the cut acts as though it were from ten to fifteen times sharper. This style of cut is particularly applicable to cutting soft substances; it is not so, on the other hand, with hard substances. For the latter a blow is required having great momentum, resulting from the velocity and the weight of the weapon.

The surgeon's bistouri and the table knife both cut by sawing, as though they were from ten to fifteen times sharper than they actually are, varying within those limits according to the nature of the tangential motion given to them.

The Mameluke scimitar, owing to its curvature, **cuts** like a straight sword of equal length and thickness, but of a breadth about four times as great, whose edges would be four times as acute.

A straight knife used with an alternate motion cuts as though, length and thickness remaining the same, its width were from ten to thirty times as great, and consequently as though its edge were from ten to thirty times as **sharp**.

Thus, when the edge is perpendicular to the stroke, it penetrates like a wedge having the same angles; but when it is oblique to the direction of motion, it penetrates as though the angle of the edge were more acute, and this effect increases with the obliquity.

This advantage may be obtained by making the blow in the ordinary direction, and with the usual velocity, but having the edge oblique (Fig. 35),* or the edge being straight, by causing it to act with a sawing motion. The latter method adds much to the effect of the pressure, and to a blow made with small normal velocity, but it is by no means applicable to cutting through aught but soft substances.

To make a sword which shall act with an edge inclined to the direction of the blow, may be effected in various ways. The blade may be straight in its general direction, the edge being cut saw-fashion, or into a flame shape, or the edge of the blade may have a general inclination to the origin of the blade.

The effect is much increased by the curvature of the blades, as in the Mameluke sabre; it is less, but still tolerably apparent in highly curved European blades; and it is insignificant in those of slight curvature, as in the last French pattern.

---

* The guillotine is a case in point, and as few persons have seen either a specimen or a drawing of this instrument, I append, at Fig. 5, a sketch of the "Axe of a Guillotine, cut down by the late Admiral Scott at Guadaloupe in 1794, at the taking of the West India Islands. Fifty Royalists had already been decapitated by it." It is preserved in the United Service Museum, Scotland Yard, and numbered 1593.   T.

It is to be remarked that it is by an analogous effect that pointed instruments endowed with a rotatory motion penetrate under pressure—as for example, screw-augers and corkscrews. The separation of the fibres caused by the point is no longer the effect of a simple cone, having an inclination in conformity with the lines of the sides of its generating angles; but rather as though this angle, having the same base, had for a side the curved line described by one of the extremities of the base, or as though this angle were very much smaller.

This further explains one of the advantages of the rifle; since a ball endowed with a rotatory motion cleaves more easily through the air, and more especially through the object struck: this being tantamount to having a greater velocity at the moment of impact; and more than this indeed, for with equal velocities, its penetration would exceed that of a musket bullet.*

5. With a sling a bullet † may be thrown with very considerable velocity, approaching to that of a musket

---

* This boring action is treated as absurd by Robuis, at p. 334 of his famous work "New Principles of Gunnery," for he says, "the rifles (grooves) of the piece diminish the velocity of the bullet, and consequently its powers of penetration." The original French work having been published in 1841, there can hardly be question of a conical bullet. Nor, according to my ideas, can the case of a fluid, like the air, be deemed analogous to a fibrous substance, like wood or flesh.

† Bullets made of lead, called in Greek *molybdides* and in Latin *glandes*, and of a form between an acorn and an almond, were cast in moulds (Lucretius and Ovid), to be thrown from slings. They have been found on the plains of Marathon and in other parts of Greece, and are remarkable for the inscriptions and devices which they exhibit, such as thunderbolts, the names of persons, and the word "DEXAI," meaning "Take this." I have measured such a gland; it was 1·18″ in length, 0·71″ in breadth, and 0·62″ in thickness, and weighed 686 grains, about the weight of our old Minié bullet.   T.

bullet fired with a small charge. This velocity is
communicated to the projectile by a motion of rotation
of the hand and of the lanyards of the sling; the
lanyards are of about the same length as a sword.
We may imagine consequently, that the edge of a
sword is capable of acquiring very great velocity, and
one almost analogous to the sling; but for this purpose
the weapon must be very light; we may likewise
observe that lightness is one of the qualities of all
swords known for their powers of cutting well. To
this end the advantage of a protective hilt is sacrificed
in the Mameluke sabres, and the British, Prussian, and
Hungarian curved swords have but a single branch to
the hilt.

In cutting with full force, the velocity of the hilt of
the sword is much less than that of the point of the
blade, precisely in the same manner as that of the
wrist whirling a sling, and of the bullet which it pro-
jects. Several foreign regulations insist on the arm
and fore-arm being almost stationary in giving certain
cuts.

Some weapons, such as battle-axes, two-handed
swords, act by means of great volume and small
velocity. If, on the one hand, they produce great
effect, on the other, they are heavy, difficult to handle,
and their system of fence is but little favourable to
vivacity of attack and defence. The nations most
famed for the use of the sword are armed with weapons
so light, that the edge attains a velocity which may
be compared to that of certain projectiles. The momentum in both cases is the same, only that in the

latter, it is composed of a light weight multiplied into a great velocity. The velocity of the point of a sword, in making a cut which produces a great effect with the edge, may be estimated perhaps at about fifty metres (164 feet) per second.

6. In the cut, a sword should be considered in the light of a projectile, of which the portion in the neighbourhood of the point has a much greater velocity than the hilt. The hand gives it this impulse, and does not act by pressing the sword on the body to be penetrated at the moment of impact.

For the velocity to be a maximum, the origin of the blade, after having traversed a large space, should be in the line of prolongation of the fore-arm.

By experiment we shall find that the portion of the blade with which the object should be struck, depends on the shape of the sword. In straight patterns it is situate at a point about two decimetres (eight inches) from the point of the blade.

At the moment of impact, the whole of the sword moves with an impulse perpendicular to the object struck, but with a velocity diminishing from point to hilt. We will examine how the different parts of the sword act.

Let us suppose (Fig. 6) the edge to strike at a distance of two decimetres (eight inches) from the point, there will be three parts of the sword acting differently, namely, the part between the spot which strikes and the point, again, the part on the other side of this spot, having an equal momentum with the former and being of about equal length; and finally, the rest of the sword between the end of the second part and that of the hilt.

The two first parts form a whole, the impulse of which acts *in equilibrio* on the point struck: let us call this whole A, the length of which is about four decimetres (sixteen inches) from the point.

The remaining portion of the sword will act agreeably to the doctrine of the decomposition of forces: we will call it R.

The examination of the effects produced by A and R is most important: we shall make some *approximate calculations* in this matter.

Let us admit, what is very near the truth, that A weighs one-fourth of the total weight, P, of the sword, and consequently one-third of the weight of R; that the velocity of the centre of gravity of A is fifty metres per second, and five times greater than that of the centre of gravity of R. The weights will be

$$\frac{P}{4} \text{ for A.}$$
$$\frac{3P}{4} \text{ for R.}$$

The velocities of the centres of gravity will be

50 metres for A.
10 metres for R.

The momenta (the weight into the velocity) will be represented—

$$\text{for A, by } \frac{P}{4} \times 50 \text{ or } P \times 12.5 ;$$
$$\text{for R, by } \frac{3P}{4} \times 10 \text{ or } P \times 7.5.$$

That is to say, that the momentum of A is to that of R in the ratio of 125 to 75, or as 5 to 3.

The momentum of A will be entirely applied to the body struck at its centre of gravity: it is not so, however, with R.

If, at the moment of impact (Fig. 5 and 6), the sword were not restrained by the hand, the part R would follow its impulse, and would tend to turn round the point struck, thus adding little force to the stroke. But if the wrist become a fulcrum, the part R will act as a lever, the fulcrum being at the wrist, the power of which will be the momentum acting at the centre of gravity, and the resistance is at the point struck, that is to say, at the centre of gravity of A. The force, placed at A, acting in the opposite direction, which would keep the impulse of R *in equilibrio*, or, in other words, the effect of R at that point, will be therefore to the momentum of R in the inverse ratio of the distances of the centres of gravity of R and A to the centre of the hilt, that is to say, in most swords nearly as 1 : 4.

Thus, not only is the momentum of A to that of R in the ratio of five to three, but further, the effect of R upon the point struck is only represented by one-fourth of its momentum. We will calculate the ratio of these effects.

The effect of A is represented by the momentum P × 12·5 the whole of which acts fully on the object struck.

The effect of R is one-fourth of the momentum P × 7·5 or P × 1·89.

The ratio of the two effects is thus—

$$\frac{P \times 12\cdot5}{P \times 1\cdot89} \text{ or } \frac{12\cdot5}{1\cdot89} \text{ or } 6\cdot6.$$

A produces consequently nearly sevenfold the useful effect of R.

Experiment confirms this train of reasoning. Thus, first, if the part A be joined to the part R by a hinge, a cut may be made almost as well as with the entire sword: second, if a sword be placed vertically *in equilibrio*, point upwards, and that the part A be struck with a stick, as though to cut the latter through, the sword will be thrown backwards, the part A with considerable velocity and the hilt much more slowly. A sort of motion of rotation round the latter as a centre takes place; third, in the axe, the metal head is the part A, R is the handle, whose weight is only just sufficient that the material may be of adequate strength. Maces and clubs are constructed on this principle.

The chief action of the sword is thus due to the last four decimetres (sixteen inches) of the blade next the point. The part A should be as heavy and be endowed with as great velocity as is possible. The rest, R, of the sword has a much inferior effect.

The necessary liveliness of the motions of attack and defence require that the weight of the sword should not exceed certain limits. On the other hand, a soldier requires a sword to be what is termed *well balanced*, that is to say, that there should be a certain ratio between the weights of the blade and hilt, such that the whole weapon should not be too heavy near the point, which would be inconvenient, nor too light, which would not admit of its inflicting a powerful blow. The centre of gravity of the sword should be at a distance from the hilt varying according to the patterns, which experiment will easily determine for each pattern.

To give a sword its whole power of cutting without altering either its weight or the position of its centre of gravity, the weight may be increased at each end and decreased in the centre, and to effect this, first the part A should be made heavy; second, the rest of the sword should be lightened as much as possible; third, the hilt should be made lighter; for instance, it might be made of steel, which will give the same amount of strength with much less weight; fourth, the pummel should be weighted. A sword thus made would be light, well balanced, and have great power of cutting.

It is to be remarked, that to move the sword in the hand, we must cause the index and little finger to act successively as fulcrum and power to re-act on the hilt and on the sword generally, as on a lever, the resistance being the whole weight applied at the centre of gravity. If the distribution of the weight of the various parts be altered without changing the position of the centre of gravity on the total weight, the resistance and its point of application will remain the same, and the sword will be equally well-balanced after the alteration in the distribution, as previous to it. We must admit, then, that the alterations above recommended are not to the prejudice of the facility of handling the sword. We may observe further, that though the sword be lightened, the amount of force required to move it in the hand may remain the same although the arm of the lever be lengthened, that is to say, that *cæteris paribus*, the lighter the sword the further its centre of gravity may be from the hilt, without prejudice to the balance of the sword.

In cutting with a straight sword, the point having as much velocity as possible, the edge impinges on the object in a normal direction, and the hand may act in two ways:

First—If it be checked suddenly, the part R contributes its decomposed forces to the stroke, reduced, as we have seen, to one-fourth of the momentum.

Second—If the hand be not checked, but prolong the motion, it produces two effects: the first is to give the blow a certain additional amount of force, which must be still further much reduced from that above calculated, as the **fulcrum** from which the forces are decomposed no longer exists; the second is due to the fact that the prolongation of the motion of the hand causes the edge to slip over the point struck, and gives it a greater faculty of penetration by making it cut as though it were much sharper.

Both methods of cutting are in use, and may be employed according to the pattern of sword, its velocity, and the nature of the object to be cut. The first system gives the more powerful blow, and the last is necessary in producing certain delicate effects. The first is prescribed in the German cavalry sword-exercise; we may add that it is that which should be generally practised, and that the second can only be of service in exceptional cases, which are more curious than useful as applied to military affairs.

In the Mameluke sabre, the part A is much longer than in straight swords, owing to its curvature; it extends as far as two-thirds of the whole length of the blade; the centre of gravity of the part R is much nearer the point than in our patterns, in consequence of the lightness of the hilt, it re-acts with greater force on the stroke, because it is situate nearer the point struck, and because its action tends, in consequence of its curve, to give the part A a sawing motion. The lightness of the scimitar admits of the part A being made heavy; further, this sword acts with an immense amount of effective momentum.

The curved British sword is very thin, but very broad at the part A, which, in conjunction with a considerable curvature, gives this weapon great capacity for cutting.

Our swords are not heavy enough at the part A; hence they strike with little percussive force, and cut badly.

In the pattern which I propose, the blade, between A and the hilt, is as narrow as possible. The hilt being made of steel, is light; the part A is broad and thick. This sword is well balanced, and with equal weight has more percussive force.

By making the edge narrower and more obtuse between the part A and the hilt, the blade is weakened. If the action of the sword were due to the force of the hand pressing it on the object, this arrangement would be of prejudicial importance; but the case is not so. The part R is not intended for cutting, but serves neither more nor less than the purpose of a handle to give the part A both velocity and direction; the great velocity is at the part A; it is here that swords break on impact; the part R is much less likely to be injured, because in that part the velocity is less and the effect of impact on the blade less sensible, as it only acts by decomposition of force.

7. The fineness of the edge has very great influence upon the effect produced by the stroke; it is as necessary to the good effect of the sword as resin is **to that** of the violin bow. We have seen how the penetrative power of the blade may be increased, and the same effect produced as though the edge were much sharper —by curving the blade, or by a sawing stroke. The fineness of the edge gains in its effect in the like proportion.

The fineness of the edge depends upon the material of which the sword is made. The first cutting arms were made of very hard wood, or of bones or stones. In the tombs of ancient warriors are found stone-arms used in war: the edge of all these arms is tolerably obtuse. Bronze and iron were far inferior to steel for this purpose. Finally, the selection and manufacture of steel for the purpose of making well-cutting sword-blades constitutes a special trade of great importance to the efficiency of this weapon. The stuff, without being brittle, should be sufficiently hard to take an edge which should be at once very fine and able to resist a blow. It is this latter quality which constitutes one of the great merits of Eastern blades. The edge can be ground very fine, and it will retain its sharpness much better than if made of more ordinary steel. As it is absolutely requisite that the edge should be capable of withstanding a blow, the nature of the material must determine its angle.

Our French swords have been much improved lat-
terly, as regards both the stuff and its temper; but
they have one great fault which may very easily be
avoided: they get soon blunted. The best-sharpened
sword, if it is drawn out of the scabbard and returned three or four times, has but a dull edge,
because it rubs in these motions against the metal of
the scabbard, especially at its mouth. As the fineness
of edge of the sword is an essential condition to efficiency in cutting, it seems to be imperatively necessary
to have battens in the scabbard which shall protect the
edge, preserving it from every species of shock or
friction against steel, in drawing and returning, and
this not only inside the scabbard but more especially
at its mouth.

8. Bodies which are intended to traverse resisting
mediums, affect peculiar forms having a certain analogy
between each other; these are dependent upon the
velocity, volume, and surface of the penetrating body,
as well as upon the nature of that penetrated. In
general terms, these forms have either a point or an
edge which cleans the body to be penetrated, a swell
the maximum thickness of which has a variable position as regards the whole length of the body, and an
end likewise terminating in a point or edge; besides
curved surfaces connecting these three portions.
Such are the forms of fish intended to move through
the water, of birds through the air, of the submerged
part of water-fowls, as well as of the sections of ships
and boats in the like situation. In no case is the
widest part situate at the end opposite to that which

forces the passage; on the contrary, it is invariably in the other half.

The greater **the velocity of penetration the more** does the length of the body increase in proportion to its width, and the more, likewise, does the extreme width approach the part which penetrates.

Generally speaking, fish are from four to five times the length of their greatest depth, and are at the same time comparatively narrow; their maximum depth and thickness are ordinarily situate at about one-fourth or one-third of their length from the head. They cleave the water in the direction of their depth, by two inclined curves, which facilitate penetration in the same manner as the curve of a sabre, acting as though the depth were less than it actually is.

The plough-share cleaves the earth and throws the sod to one side; to effect this, the plough-share has one part which cuts vertically, a second which cuts horizontally, and a third which displaces the earth cut and throws it out of the furrow. The latter is not flat like the face of a wedge; it is curvilinear in form, after the same fashion and with the same object as is the right side of the submerged portion of the bow of a boat.

Judiciously made arrows have a swell in the shaft; the latter, instead of being cylindrical, increases in thickness from the point to about one-third of the length, and thence diminishes to the end.

There would be, doubtless, less eddy caused by the piers of bridges, and less action of the water thereon, if their horizontal section, instead of being a rectangle rounded at both ends, were shaped more like that appropriate to the submerged part of a boat cutting through the water at the same velocity as that of the current.

If Congreve rockets were shaped agreeably to this idea, they would meet with less resistance from the air. I am not aware whether there may not be other considerations opposed to the adoption of this form.

The shape of a bullet or of a round-shot is not that best adapted for penetrating the air and the object fired at; but it is necessitated by other cogent reasons. But for these, projectiles ought to cleave the air by a point; their thickness should then increase up to a certain distance, whence they should slope away until they ended in another point. They would thus lose less velocity from the resistance of the air, and with equal velocities would penetrate deeper into the object struck.

I think that in certain cases rifles might carry projectiles of the above-described form. We know that a bullet projected by an arm of this nature moves with the part struck by the ramrod invariably forwards through the whole of the trajectory. If a Tyrolese rifle be loaded and the ball afterwards extracted, we shall find on examination that it is still spherical on the side next the powder—that it has become cylindrical and marked with a few grooves at the part which was in contact with the sides of the bore—and that it is flattened on the side struck by the ramrod. This shape is but little adapted for penetration, and it

would be preferable that the flattened portion intended
to cleave the air and the object should be made conical
—an arrangement which might be easily enough
effected by coning out the end of the ramrod. The
latter suggestion is, however, by no means applicable
to heavy rifles which throw bullets from six to eight
to the pound. It would be necessary that the bullet
should be of the usual calibre and of the same weight,
but should be elongated in form, ending in a point
anteriorly. Not only would the projectile, under
these circumstances, have a greater force of penetration, but these heavy rifles might be loaded
with the ordinary cartridge—a matter of no small
advantage.

We may account for the peculiar shape of these
penetrating bodies by the following considerations :—

When one body penetrates another, it may act
either by tearing, cutting, or carrying away with it
whatever may be opposed to its course. Thus, let
us suppose a cloth stretched on a frame, a stone
thrown by the hand will traverse it by tearing, a
stroke with the edge of the sword by cutting, and a
musket-bullet will make a hole through it of its own
diameter.

When a round-shot strikes sand or stones, we per-
ceive that these substances are driven with great
velocity, which frequently renders them dangerous.

The same effect takes place when a round-shot rico-
chets on water.

If a round shot penetrate into water, it should
likewise in its course drive the liquid opposed to it

before it, the shock of which ought to be serious to a living creature immersed in the water in the neighbourhood of the trajectory of the projectile. In the air, an analogous effect takes place, producing what is termed the "*wind of the shot.*" I have been enabled to satisfy myself on this point, during experiments carried on with twenty-four pounders firing large charges. If at ten metres (thirty-three feet) from the muzzle, the shot pass from one to two centimetres (0·39—0·79 inch) above a glass full of water, it was emptied; over a frog, it was killed; above an apple, and it was softened as it would have been under great pressure.[*]

[*] I have always looked upon this question of the effect of the wind of a shot, as a most difficult one to form a satisfactory opinion upon. One author supports the idea that it is dangerous to the human frame; while, on the other hand, I have read in medical books that portions of the dress of sailors and marines, on board men-of-war, have been carried away by round-shot fired at close quarters, without injury to the wearers. I have further heard related, by a personal friend, a circumstantial account of an officer engaged at Sobraon being turned black and blue by the same cause; and, *per contra*, it is an undoubted fact, that Brigadier Russell, of H.M.'s 84th Foot, had a gold chain cut in two by a round-shot at the back of his neck, without sustaining further injury than that resulting from a fall on the occasion, due to the peculiarity of the local position in which he was standing. The cases stated by the author are staggering enough; but what are we to conclude from the following experiment?—

"The fact that a cannon ball, passing close by a living subject, exercises lateral pressure on the air sufficient to produce a contusion, has often been asserted, and as often denied. On this disputed matter M. E. Pélikan, of St. Petersburgh, has just presented a paper to the Academy of Sciences of Paris, giving an account of certain experiments, instituted with a view to set the question at rest. Having obtained the concurrence of the Russian Government, M. Pélikan caused a cylinder of sheet-iron, one foot in diameter, to be constructed, with a piston moving easily inside. The piston-rod was provided at its outer extremity with a black-lead pencil, to mark the recoil on a slip of paper. The whole apparatus was firmly fixed on a strong wooden frame. The piston and piston-rod weighed 8 lb., and a force of 1¼ lb. was requisite to make the piston-rod recoil an inch. At four metres (13 feet) distance from the frames a wooden screen was erected, in order to ascertain the distance of the projectile from the piston at the

The above effects are identical with those obtained by discharging an air-gun containing a great quantity of compressed air, but without a bullet, against the same objects; if the air-gun be discharged against the flesh at a distance of one centimetre (0·39 inch) it brings blood. A round-shot moving with great velocity, and passing very close to a man, should cause a very dangerous shock, the effect of which would increase with the calibre.

If a musket be discharged so that the bullet strike the flat of a book, the projectile acts by tearing, if it

moment of its passage. Although the experiments instituted in 1843 and 1844 in the Arsenal of Washington, by Ensign Mordecai, proved that at the distance of 48 feet the gases emanating from the powder have no effect upon the ballistic pendulum ; a second screen was placed before the other at a distance of five metres (16 feet) from the apparatus, in order to protect it, if necessary, from the action of these gases. A 40 lb. howitzer (7·7 inches calibre) was then placed at a distance of 14 metres (46 feet) from the first screen, the charge of powder being 4 lb. ; the velocity of the projectile at that distance was equal to that of a bomb-shell projected with a 7 lb. charge—viz., 956 feet per second. The results obtained showed : 1, that at a distance of three inches, the piston remained immoveable ; 2, that even when the projectile broke off a part of the wooden frame supporting the iron cylinder, the piston gave no indication of motion ; 3, but that if the projectile just grazed the surface of the piston, a recoil of two inches was obtained ; 4, if, on the other hand, a fragment of the frame hit the cylinder, the piston, instead of moving backwards, would move forwards about 3½ lines ; 5, if the cylinder, instead of being placed parallel to the screens, was placed obliquely, a recoil would take place of from one-quarter to one-half of an inch. Hence M. Pélikan concludes that since the piston required a force of 1½lb. in order to be moved one inch, and the wind of a cannon-ball can never be expected to exercise such a force, the passage of a projectile close to a living subject will only produce an insignificant effect, which cannot amount to a contusion."—Extract from the *Times* newspaper.

The conclusion come to by the experimenter is doubtless justified, and, so far as it goes, is perfectly satisfactory ; but it would have been desirable had the description been a little more lucid as to the position of the cylinders and piston in each case, and that the piece of ordnance had been a long gun giving a velocity of 1600 feet per second.   T.

does not pass through it; but if its velocity be sufficient to carry it through, it clears a passage; the orifice is of a diameter equal to the calibre of the bullet, while the exit is from about twice to thrice that diameter; because the portions carried forward by the bullet are driven with great velocity, and thus become projectiles themselves: so that at the exit the effect is more than double—due to the bullet and the parts of the object carried before it.

It is remarkable that with high velocities soft substances and even liquids can pierce through hard bodies; thus, with wax, tallow, grease, or water, a board may be traversed by firing them from a musket from a short distance;—these experiments I have myself made. Penetration, in such case, takes place, because there is a certain volume combined with velocity and adequate condensation. But when the distance is much increased, these bodies no longer penetrate, by default of velocity and more particularly in consequence of diffusion, water being reduced to spray. Further, certain sportsmen load their guns with water instead of dust-shot, so as to kill birds without injuring their plumage.

In cutting a branch off a tree by a very swift blow of a sword, the portion so cut off is endowed with a certain velocity, which usually carries it to the distance of a metre (3·3 feet). The cause and effect in this case are identical with the above.

A round-shot traversing certain sorts of timber, if the velocity be high, makes a passage for itself without carrying away the piece. After the shot has passed,

there is no hole in the timber. The fibres of the wood
separate, and then close in again.

In this last case the effect approaches closely to that
which takes place in striking with cutting weapons;
the velocity causes the edge to penetrate; the blade
enters the wound by thrusting aside the parts divided,
while these again close in; if the blade be in the shape
of a wedge—if its greatest thickness be at the back—
the divided parts, in closing in again, press against the
blade and diminish the amount of penetration. If, on
the other hand, the blade be shaped so that its thickness diminishes from the neighbourhood of the cutting
edge to the back, and that this edge, on coming in contact with the object, be sufficiently sharp to produce
adequate incision; and again—if, in the combination
of the two motions, the penetration of the sword and
the resistance of the parts, the latter do not take place
until the blade has passed, the result should be that
there would be no pressure or friction exerted on the
blade, excepting in the part near the edge where it
cannot be avoided; consequently, the amount of penetration would be greater with a blade so shaped than
with a wedge-shaped blade.

The blow of a man acts by contusion or laceration;
the edge of a sword, by incision only. The point acts
by incision and separation. The vertex of the angle
having penetrated, the edges, if they be sharp, divide
the substance by incision, while the thickness of the
side faces acts by separation. If the point be blunt at
both edges, it penetrates by separation.

Some much-improved patterns of Oriental **sabres**

are formed in a manner which seems to be the application of the above remarks. The greatest thickness of the blade is not at the back, but about mid-way or one-third way from the edge, whence it gradually diminishes towards the back.* There are some few European swords (Fig. 7) which already cut well, susceptible of improvement in the above manner.

The principle admits, further, of application to arms intended for pointing. The edges of the metal, connecting the point with the back and cutting-edge, should not form abrupt angles at the points of junction; it is evident, further, that they should not be in the same straight line; these edges should, consequently, form curves commencing at the point and running away into the lines of the back and cutting-edge. Experiment, indeed, proves, in trying swords of both shapes, that the latter penetrate with by far the greater facility.

9. The object of the sword-knot is to prevent the sword from dropping completely, in the case of its being knocked out of the hand. It is easy to compass

---

* The Translator saw a sword, evidently of the pattern alluded to, in Turkey, in 1853. A sketch of it is given at Fig. 7. The owner, a Turkish officer, valued it at 7000 piastres (about £50). He said it was of Baghdad manufacture, that the steel was of the quality termed "Taban," and that its shape was called "Bala." It certainly was the handiest weapon ever the Translator held; its power of cutting was evidently enormous, and it had but one trifling disadvantage, namely, the preposterous size and shape of the scabbard, the back of which was open down to the first ring, about three inches. In the United Service Museum, Scotland Yard, London, may be found two specimens of this sort of sabre, but vastly inferior in finish and value to the one above-described : viz., "Nos. 810 and 811—Turkish Pirate Sabres, presented by Lieut. G. W. Roberts, R.A." The length of the blade, measured along the chord of its curve, was 27 inches.

this object, without injuring the capacity of the sword for cutting; this cannot be said of our sword-knot. 1st. It is too stiff, thick, and heavy, and has too much swing in consequence of the weight of the end; it is inconvenient, and but little used; the trooper prefers a handkerchief rolled up, which weighs little, and is, further, supple and convenient. 2nd. It is fastened to the hilt at the spot where the little finger bears, and seriously impedes its action.

In the Mameluke scimitar, the sword-knot is made of silk; it is very light and thin, and is attached to the sword by being passed through a hole bored in the hilt in a direction perpendicular to the flat of the blade, and in the centre of the rounded part whereon the little fingers bears.* The object is thus attained without being attended with any injurious effect.

Our sword-knot should be made of silk or goat's hair; it should be about three millimetres (0·12 inch) in thickness; it should, further, have a light sliding-loop, and the end should be a simple knot without an acorn; nor should it be fastened to the main branch, but to the next one—by which arrangement it would be impossible for it to interfere with the bearing of the little finger. I look upon this matter as by no means unimportant to the efficiency of the cut.

10. In former days swords were worn horizontally, and this is still the custom among certain nations. To hang thus, it is requisite to have two billets which will keep the sheath in that position, being attached

---

* Vide Fig. 1, for the Turkish sword-knot and the manner of attaching it to the hilt.

thereto in such a manner that the centre of gravity of
the sword and scabbard shall be situate between the
two points of attachment. In Europe, since the
middle of the last century, the sabre and sword are
worn by being hung vertically; one billet alone is
actually of use—it is that which is fastened to the
scabbard above the centre of gravity. The second
billet has, however, been retained; of it we may say,
that it is unnecessary, of no utility, and that it entails
the following disadvantageous circumstances: 1st.
The band to which the ring is attached seriously injures the shabracque by striking against it in consequence of the motion of the horse. 2nd. This same
band frequently catches under the quarter of the saddle
in the Heavy Cavalry at a trot, producing a jerk which
drags the rider downwards in a very unpleasant manner.
3rd. When the trooper is mounted the greater billet
forms a long loose bight. It consequently frequently
catches some portion of the neighbouring rider's ac-
coutrements or dress; the spur of the latter has been
known to catch in it with the chance of a serious acci-
dent. At all events, it is the cause of injury and
disorder. This is more especially the case when going
at a fast pace, and coming about by fours or by troops.
4th. For the above reason, it frequently catches on the
valise and incommodes the trooper in dismounting.
It has happened, too, that a man having been thrown,
he has thus been dragged by his horse while running
away. 5th. It sometimes gets between the saddle and
the horseman. 6th. It cannot be said that if the short
billet break the long billet would support the sword;

for in such a case it would hang hilt downwards, the
sword would come out of the scabbard and fall to the
ground.   7th. The point where the long billet is fastened to the waist-belt is the cause of grievous inconvenience in such corps as wear the belt over the coat;
this point should be placed between the two waist-
buttons behind; the thickness of a man's waist varies
according to his condition and the clothes he has on;
the position of the short billet at the left side is inva-
riable; if, then, the long billet be sewed on the waist-
belt, it would be necessary to shift the swing whenever
the circumference of the man's waist altered, in order
that the long billet might still be between the two
buttons: to avoid this, it has **become necessary to
attach a strap to the lower side of the waist-belt along**
which the loop of the long billet may run.

To recapitulate : the long billet is a useless weight,
a troublesome bit of gear, hurtful and sometimes dangerous. It seems to be only rational that it, together
with its band and ring on the scabbard, should be
abolished.

CHAPTER II.

RECAPITULATION OF THE PRINCIPLES INVOLVED IN
ARMS USED FOR CUTTING.

THE peculiar conditions which are involved in the
fact of a sword cutting will seem to be the following :—

First—That part of the hilt whereon the little finger
bears should be wide and smooth.

Second—The grip should be smooth, and nothing

should be allowed to impede the **action of the** index and little fingers.

Third—The grip should be as narrow as possible in the direction of from back to edge of the blade, especially where it is grasped by the index and little fingers.

Fourth—In cutting, the thumb should not be placed on the back of the grip.

Fifth—If the guard of the hilt be not symmetrical, its main branch should be stout, and placed, not in the centre, but on the side opposite to the other two.

Sixth—The hilt should be light, and consequently it would be well if it were made of iron or steel; the pummel should be slightly loaded with metal.

Seventh—The triangle which forms the edge should be increased in height in that part of the blade which **comes in contact with the object.**

Eighth—The curvature of the blade has the effect of giving the sword a finer edge. This effect is very marked in the Mameluke sabre; it is imperceptible in slightly curved blades. The same effect is attained by the flame-shaped blade, by a serrated edge, by sliding **the edge on the wound, termed "sawing."**

Ninth—The velocity has a great effect on the stroke, and consequently the same may be said of the lightness of the sword.

Tenth—The lighter the sword the further may **the** centre **of** gravity be placed from the hilt without destroying the balance.

Eleventh—The last four decimetres (sixteen inches) next the point is the part which acts in cutting, and is much more effective on impact with the object than the rest of the arm. **Unless the** blade have a peculiar power owing to curvature, this portion of it should be thick for the sword to have great percussive force.

Twelfth—For a straight sword to have great percussive force, and to be at the same time light **and well** balanced, the last four decimetres (sixteen **inches) next** the point must be thick; the remainder of the **blade** should be light, and have its centre of gravity towards the pummel, which, consequently, should be slightly loaded.

Thirteenth—The fineness of the cutting-edge is of the greatest importance for a sword to cut well. **The** steel must be well tempered, it must take a very fine edge, and be at the same time sufficiently strong to resist a blow. The scabbard should be so made that it shall not dull a well-sharpened edge; it should be consequently lined with wooden battens reaching up to its mouth.

Fourteenth—The greatest thickness of blade in the part intended for cutting should not be at the back, **but between it and the** cutting-edge, at a distance dependent upon the velocity of the stroke. This improvement is more applicable to swords which are specially intended for cutting.

Fifteenth—The sword-knot should be light, supple, and without a big or heavy acorn end; it should be fastened to the middle branch of the hilt, so as not to incommode the little finger. It should be made either of silk or goat's hair, instead of leather.

Sixteenth—The long billet of the sword-belt, as well as the band and ring on the scabbard, should be abolished.

CHAPTER III.

EXAMINATION OF THE ACTION OF CERTAIN ARMS AND
TOOLS USED FOR CUTTING.

FROM what has been above stated, we may be able to
appreciate the merits and demerits of certain arms and
tools used for cutting.

The Mameluke sabre has a smooth grip, **narrow**
in the direction of from front to back of the blade;
the part upon which the little finger bears is very
broad; the hilt has no guard so as to be light; the
grip is narrow in all directions in the neighbourhood
of the blade—thence it increases in dimensions towards the pummel; the weapon is symmetrical with
reference to the plane of the blade; the latter, owing
to its shape, is strong, defends well, and has a great
power of cut, to which the immense velocity with
which it can be wielded, owing to its lightness, notably
contributes. This sabre is well balanced, and yet its
centre of gravity is distant from the hilt; in consequence of the excellence of the stuff of which it is
made, it takes a very keen edge capable of resisting
a stroke by the real angle of its edge, while it cuts as
though that angle were much more acute. The greatest
thickness of the blade is not at the back; its scabbard
preserves the fineness of its edge; the sword-knot is
light and judiciously attached to the hilt. This weapon
strikes with the velocity of a projectile, and takes by
surprise—so to speak—any light object, in the same
manner that a bullet would pierce a delicately hung

weathercock; it is, at the same time, capable of producing surprising effects on resisting bodies. The
Mameluke sabre embodies combination of qualities
such that it may be said to be perfection; it is impossible to imagine any improvement in it; as a cutting
weapon, it is a *chef d'œuvre*, like the Tyrolese rifle
among fire-arms.

The curved British sword (Fig. 2) has likewise great
capacity for cutting; the grip and hilt are well constructed, but the sword-knot is attached at the bearing
of the little finger, which is injudicious. The blade is
of good steel and well tempered; it has great percussive force, is light, and takes a fine edge. **This**
weapon is inferior to the Mameluke sabre in cutting
moderately soft substances: much more so for delicate
strokes, such as cutting a handkerchief in the air, or
a sheet of paper placed flat on the table; but it is perhaps superior to it in its effect on hard substances, such
as cutting the ashen shaft of a lance—that is to say,
when the stroke should fall like an axe to avoid friction. This sword would be more powerful, perhaps,
if the blade were lightened from the grip to the part
A, and made heavier at the cutting part. If, with these
alterations, it were not well balanced, although light,
the grip might be weighted at the pummel. The
cutting part should be thickest about mid-way across
the breadth, and not at the back. The British sword,
as a European arm, has the fault of being in no way
calculated for thrusting.

Our present light cavalry sword (Fig. 45) has several
faults above exposed as to the hilt, grip, and sword-

knot. We may add that not only does the hilt injure the little finger in the act of cutting, but that the copper wire on the grip impedes that motion, and that "moulinets"* being practised for a few minutes, suffices to wear a hole in the glove, or to injure the hand. Its curvature is too small to have any perceptible effect; its percussive force is feeble in consequence of the lightness of the cutting part. The scabbard destroys the fineness of edge.

The old light cavalry sword termed "Bancal" † has a portion of the same faults ; its curvature being greater, however, its power of cut is increased, and of thrust decreased. Its percussive force is greater, consequent upon the width and thickness of the blade at the part which acts in cutting.

The horse-artillery sword (Fig. 46) is short, heavy-hilted, and light at the part A; it thrusts very badly, in consequence of its curvature, and cuts badly because it has little percussive force. A straight sword of the same length, made as above described as regards the blade, and having a wide bearing for the little finger at the hilt, would cut and thrust very much better.

Several patterns of heavy cavalry swords, intended

* Vide note, p. 7. T.
† This word means "bandy-legged," and is applied familiarly to this particular sword, owing to its curvature probably. Most of the weapons in use in the French service have similar nicknames. The short, straight, infantry sword, intended to be used as a fascine-knife, goes by the soubriquet of "coupe choux" (cabbage-cutter). (Fig. 48). The old infantry sword in Napoleon the First's time, and still in use in some corps (Fig. 47), was called a "Briquet" (a steel for striking fire by a flint), &c. So in like manner with us, an infantry officer's sword is facetiously termed "a spit," or "a bread-earner," both of which names it seems to deserve, but for different reasons. T.

to be used exclusively for thrusting, have a blade
with three blunt edges, the latter being intended
to give it rigidity. The angle of the cutting edge is
consequently **very obtuse**, and the sword but little
adapted for cutting. It is thence, I think, that arises
the erroneous idea that straight swords never cut well.

The present heavy cavalry sword has the same defects
as that of the light cavalry.

The old infantry "Briquet" (Fig. 47) has a hilt
faulty as to weight, size, and the sharp edges of the
surface on which the little finger bears. The blade is
tolerably good for cutting with; but with the same
weight, a much better weapon could be made.

The infantry officer's sword has not only a bearing
for the little finger, but thereon are certain ornamental
ridges (the same ornament exists on the cavalry officer's
sword, constituting in both cases, a most important
defect); the hilt is not symmetrical, the grip is not
smooth, the blade has little percussive force, the
curvature but slightly augments the power of cut; it
should be supplied with a sword-knot.

The whole of the last-mentioned swords appear to
me to be easily susceptible of improvement by the
application of the above detailed principles.

Tools used for cutting differ from arms used for the
like purpose, as the latter require to be light to admit
of rapid motion in attack and defence,—to be shaped
for defence,—to be strong enough to be proof against
violent blows,—to reach to a distance—and finally, to
be conveniently portable in a scabbard.

We shall see that incisive power is conferred on edge

tools—first, by pressure, or by well distributed weight combined with velocity; second, by fineness of edge, increased in some instances by the obliquity of the direction of penetration.

Billhooks, sickles, hedging-bills and scythes have all sharp edges, the action of which is increased by obliquity of penetration, producing the effect of an edge from two to four times sharper than it actually is.

The carpenter's plane is large as to mass, and its cutting edge is oblique.

Our species of pickaxe has its cutting edges drawn to a point in the centre, in order that it may penetrate the better by cutting obliquely.

The butcher's knife cuts by an alternating motion, similar to sawing, while his cleaver, analogous in its whole length to the part A of the sword, acts without the effect of curvature.

Some axes combine great momentum with oblique penetration of the cutting edge.

In certain foreign states the headsman makes use of a long straight sword, which is heavy, broad, and sharp; it is wielded in both hands, and strikes at a short distance from the hilt; it acts afterwards by a drawing motion up to the point. The velocity is feeble, the mass great, and the effect of the cutting edge thus much increased.

Elsewhere, a short, heavy, wide, and highly curved sword is made use of, requiring but little dexterity.

An equal amount of momentum, and an equal augmentation of the effect of the cutting edge, are likewise obtainable with light swords, made wide at the part A, and highly curved. The velocity compensates for the want of mass; such swords require dexterity in their use.

There are, further, certain swords used for capital punishment, which are straight and light; one decimetre (four inches) wide near the end, and very thin at the part A; they act consequently with the same power of cutting as the Mameluke sabre, but they are too weak to be used in combat.

The yataghan, (Fig. 34,) the instrument used in executions in the East, acts by the weight of the part A, and the velocity due to the lightness of the weapon. Its curvature does not assist in the cut.

I have seen an instrument used for the same purpose, like a Mameluke sabre, but broad and thick; the hilt and the neighbouring parts are replaced by a long wooden handle adapted along the back of the blade. It is wielded in both hands, and has great power of cutting.

The instrument used in capital punishment in France, (Fig. 35,) acts like a plane, by its great mass combined with a moderate velocity and a cutting edge oblique to the direction of the stroke. The combination, however, of the three is but indifferently arranged.

PART II.

ON ARMS USED FOR THRUSTING.

CHAPTER I.

DISCUSSION OF THE PRINCIPLES INVOLVED IN ARMS USED FOR THRUSTING.

THE object of arms of this nature is to cause the point to penetrate as deeply as possible into the body struck. Let us examine the circumstances necessary to compass this object.

1. The point may penetrate either from simple pressure of the wrist, or merely by the velocity with which the weapon is moving, or by the combination of these two forces; herein it differs from the edge, which generally penetrates simply by the velocity of the sword. Consequently, in a weapon used for thrusting only, lightness is not so absolutely necessary; its weight is merely determined by what is requisite for rapidity of movement in attack and defence.

2. For the thrusting stroke, it is requisite that the blade should be rigid, so as not to break or to lose a portion of the impulse by bending.

To obtain this rigidity of blade, divers means have been employed, nearly all based on a great thickness of metal; thus :

1st. One method was to give the blade three edges, on each side, (Fig. 8,) one towards the back, another in the centre, and one towards the cutting edge; the latter was consequently very obtuse. This weapon is light, rigid enough, and little qualified for cutting.

2nd. Another (Fig. 9) is to increase the thickness of the metal at the back, and decrease its width, so that the total weight remains the same; its rigidity is moderate, and the weapon cuts better.

3rd. Another (Fig. 10) is to make a highly projecting edge at one side of the blade; this sword is very light and rigid; but it is little calculated for cutting, as much for want of symmetry as from the surface which this lateral projecting edge opposes to penetration.

4th. Lastly the blade has been made (Fig. 11) with three edges symmetrically situated, as is the case in certain short swords; an arrangement which gives great rigidity and lightness, at the complete sacrifice, however, of the power of cutting,

It seems to me that greater rigidity is obtainable, by making the back very thick without prejudice to the power of cutting, and that by way of getting rid of the excessive weight consequent thereon, the back might be fluted. I have had blades made up on this plan and of very many differing patterns. I consider the arrangement very judicious. It has moreover this advantage, that the process of fluting the back being carried out after the blade is hardened, the edge retains the proper degree of hardness, while the back being slightly tempered by the grindstone becomes less brittle.

3. The stroke with the point is of two kinds. Thus with a lance, every portion of its mass moves in a direct and parallel line. The resultant of all these forces passes through the points, which has consequently communicated to it the total amount of the existing momentum.

The point of the battle-axe, on the other hand, only acquires the direct impulse of the volume of the metal head, while that of the handle is only communicated to it by the decomposition of the forces involved.

The sword is attended with analogous effects. In pointing in tierce agreeably to the regulations, it is just possible that the whole impulse of the weapon may have the resultant of the parallel forces passing through the point. But in the position of " Guard "* of the broadsword exercise on foot, the point of the sword is higher than the wrist, and is not directed at the breast of the opponent. To thrust it is necessary to advance the wrist and lower the point, so that the different parts of the sword move with different velocities and in different directions. Swords should vary in shape according to the habitual use of the former or latter system of pointing.

Let us imagine (Fig. 12) a rectangular blade having a sharp edge at one of its lesser sides, to be pushed vertically against a horizontal surface intended to be penetrated by the cutting edge—like a carpenter's

* The words here in the original are "en garde," and the position appears by the context to correspond to the "Inside Guard" of our infantry sword-exercise. I regret not being able at this moment to refer to the French sword-exercise, to satisfy the reader and self on this point.

chisel, upon the head of which a blow is struck with a
mallet. The resistance sustained will depend on the
angle of the edge, on the force actuating it, and on
the hardness of the substance to be penetrated. If the
edge of the blade bearing on the surface be inclined,
instead of being perpendicular, to its long side as in a
plane iron (Fig. 13), the resistance met with will be
diminished. The greater the inclination of the edge,
the better will it penetrate ; for, among other reasons,
this inclination will give it the effect of being proportionately sharper, as is the case with the cutting
edge of a curved sabre.

Let us suppose that the edge forms an angle of forty
degrees with the long side of the blade (Fig. 14) ; let us
compare its power of penetration with that of a blade
(Fig. 15) whose edges, instead of being in the plane of
one of the sides, forms a salient angle of forty degrees,
symmetrical as regards the long faces of the blade,
admitting in both cases that the impulse is in the
vertical direction, or in that of the long side of the
blade. The tool having the edge in the centre will
penetrate better than that having it at the side,
because the two faces of the edge of the former will
act at angles of twenty degrees with the direction of
the blow, while the edge placed at one side of the tool
will act at an angle of forty degrees, thus having less
cutting power.

If in the second of the above supposed cases (Fig.
16) the direction of impulse still pass through the edge,
but from a direction exterior to its angle, although
contained in the **same plane** as the blade, penetration

would take place as though the angle at the apex were
the sum of the angles contained between the two faces
plus the angle contained between the direction of
impulse and the face nearest thereto.

4. If the resultant of the forces of impulse do not pass
through the apex (Fig. 17), there will ensue a decomposition of forces, one part tending to drive the edge
into the surface, and the other to cause the blade to
turn around it.

When the edge is at one side of the blade (Fig. 18),
the inclination of the face of the edge occasions a
decomposition of forces during penetration; the
resistance of the body to be penetrated acts in a
direction normal to the surface, and likewise in a tangential one; the latter force tends to cause a deviation
in the direction of the centre of that side of the tool on
which the edge is situated.

When the edge is in the centre (Fig. 19), the act of
penetration engenders two equal forces of deviation in
opposite directions, which destroy each other. The
point consequently does not deviate from the direction
of the stroke, and has a greater chance of penetrating
deeply.

If the blades be thicker on one side than the other
(Fig. 20), in order that the edges may not deviate from
the line of direction of the impulse of the blow, it
would seem that the point should be in the lines containing the centres of gravity of horizontal sections of
the blade.

From the above it appears that the most favourable
conditions for penetration of the point are, that its

angle should be a minimum, and that the line of
impulse of the force should bisect that angle. The
more the line of impulse deviates from this direction
the less is the facility of penetration; if it passes out-
side the point, there results a still greater loss of
force.

5. The smaller the mark of penetration made by
the blade, the fewer the obstacles to be overcome, and
the deeper, consequently, should be the penetration
with a given impulse. The wound will be the more
dangerous, not only by reason of its depth, but
further because of the internal bleeding which is
likely to ensue from a wound of small aperture.
The wound, then, should only be of the same dimensions, as far as possible, as the part of the blade which
inflicts it.

Let us imagine (Fig. 21) a horizontal wheel revolving
round a vertical axis, and that a blade be attached to
the end of a radius, the flat of the blade being
horizontal with its back next the axis; when the wheel
is in motion the point of the sword will describe a
circle. If the blade have the same curvature as, and
be placed on the circumference of, this circle, when it
penetrates an object in consequence of the motion of
the wheel, it will inflict a wound in the shape of an
arc of a circle, of equal length, width, and depth with
the blade. The aperture of this wound will be like a
transverse section of the blade.

If a straight blade (Fig. 22) bearing upon the end
of the circular blade be applied thereto so as to form
the chord of the arc, the wound made by the former

consequent upon the motion of the wheel will be of a
depth increased by the height of the arc.

If the circular blade (Fig. 23) has reversed in position
so as to have the original point of the blade still in the
arc of motion, but the convexity in the opposite
direction, and forming a curve with that of the original
position of the blade symmetrical about the line
joining the two points which are identical in both
cases, the wound made by the motion of the wheel
will have a depth equal to double that made by the
straight blade.

If the origin of the blade (Fig. 24) remaining in the
same situation, the point take other positions in the
horizontal plane of the limb of the wheel, the wound
would be of a depth equal to the difference of the radii
proceeding to the point and origin of the blade
(Fig. 25). The most unfavourable * case would be
that in which the blade was situate in the line of the
radius, in which case the depth would be equal to
the length of the blade.

In the case where the point describes a circle as
above, where the blade buries itself completely in the
object, and when the force is derived rather from an
exterior impulse than from a velocity, the shape and
position of the sword most favorable to penetration are
thus determined; the blade should follow the same
line of curvature described by the point and the apex
of the point should be in the line of the middle of the
blade.

* Vide the conclusion of the first paragraph of article 5 of this chapter
for the explanation of the word "unfavourable," as used here.

If we imagine a sword (Fig. 26) to fall vertically and
by the sole action of gravity, so that it has merely the
impulse due to the velocity, its action will be represented by its motive power having a vertical direction
and passing through the centre of gravity of the blade;
to penetrate deeply, the point of the blade should be
situate in this line and should be divided thereby into
two equal parts; the blade should be straight and
vertical like the line described by the points. If the
blade bury itself completely, the dimensions of the
wound will be the same as those of the blade which
inflicts it (Fig. 27). If the blade were curved, and
the line of impulse passed through the point, the
latter would deviate from the straight line in consequence of the want of symmetry in the two cutting
edges which effect the penetration, the wound would
be wide and the point would not reach to so great a
depth. (Something of this sort occurs in shoeing a
horse; the point of the curved nail traces a curvilinear
path through the hoof, the direction of which was
originally normal to that of the surface to be penetrated, but which subsequently deviates from this
direction and finally meets the lateral surface of the
hoof. (Fig. 28). If the line of impulse do not pass
through the point, there would ensue a decomposition
of force, one part of which would tend towards
causing the blade to turn around its extremity at the
moment of contact.

If the blade be pushed in connection with a block of
wood (Fig. 29) moving in a straight line, like a
carpenter's plane, and that it penetrate a body without

any deviation whatever, in order that it should meet with a minimum resistance, the blade should be straight and lie in a direction not only parallel to the straight line traced by the centre of gravity of the whole arrangement, but further, that its line of direction should contain that point. The wound would then be of the same dimension as the blade (Fig. 30). If the sword were curved, both ends of the blade should be situated in the same line of impulse, the breadth of the wound would be increased by the altitude of the curve of the blade.

If the blade (Fig. 31) moving in a straight line and constantly remaining parallel to its original position, have not its two extremities situated on a parallel to the line of impulse, the breadth of the wound would be equal to the distances between the two parallels to that line, drawn from either extremity of the blade (Fig. 32). This distance would become equal to the length of the blade, if the extremities of the latter were situated on a perpendicular to the line of impulse.

Thus, when the impulse is rectilinear, the penetration of the blade will, *cæteris paribus*, be a maximum when the sword is straight and placed in the direction of the stroke.

Let us now suppose a block of wood to move horizontally and in a straight line, like a carpenter's plane; and that this block has an horizontal axis perpendicular to the direction of motion; and finally to this axis is attached a sword (Fig. 33) by the pummel in a perpendicular direction, with its flat vertical. This sword would be capable of motion around the axis in the

vertical plane lying in the direction of the horizontal
motion of the block. If the block be stationary, every
point of the sword will describe a circle when the blade
turns round the axis. If the blade remain fixed on
the axis, and that the block move in a straight line,
every point of the sword will describe a straight line.
If the block moves rectilineally, and the sword at the
same time move in a circle round the axis, and if each
of these motions have the same velocity, each point of
the sword will trace a cycloïd. If the blade, consequent upon the impulse, penetrate without deviation
into a soft body, the point will describe a cycloïd
therein ; and that the wound should be as near as possible of the same dimensions as the sword, the latter
should be curved analogously to the cycloïd. (A
wound is like the sheath of a sword ; it cannot resemble
the form of the blade, unless the latter be straight or
circular.)

If the blade were straight, the wound would be the
wider by about the height of the cycloïd.

If the blades were of a cycloïdal form, symmetrical to
the former with reference to the two ends, the wound
would be double the width of the preceding.

The smaller the velocity of rotation in proportion
to that of rectilineal progression, the flatter would be
the cycloïd, approaching to a straight line. Its concavity, under all circumstances, will be turned towards
the line of rectilineal impulse passing through the
axis ; and if the blades were curved in the inverse
way, the difficulty of penetration would be nearly
doubled.

As a general principle we deduce the following :—
*The part of the blade which penetrates should have, as
near as possible, a form analogous to the line described
by the point of the blade.*

6. The preceding considerations will explain the
reasons of divers forms of tools, arms, and means of
defence of animals; thus the metal of the pick-axe and
mattock, as well as that of the point of the battle-axe,
is curved, because penetration takes place consequent
upon a motion of rotation. The fangs of the carnivora
act by turning round the point of junction of the jaw-
bones as on an axis; their curvature gives them a
greater power of penetration than if they were straight.
It is precisely the same with the long, hollow, frail, and
venomous fangs of the viper.

The elephant and wild boar, which wound by rushing
forwards and making a stroke of the head upwards,
cause their tusks to describe a species of cycloïd; their
tusks affect very nearly that form. The same may be
said of claws, the points of which act by a double
motion.

The sword- and saw-fishes precipitate themselves
upon their enemies swimming in a straight line; their
weapons of offence are straight, and lie in a direction
which, if prolonged, would probably pass through the
centre of gravity of those creatures.

Among our arms which act by the point, there are
some in which the latter moves in a straight line, and
others in which it moves in a curved line. Thus, in
the cavalry, all the points laid down in the regulations
are given in a straight line. In the sword-exercise on

foot it is not so : in the position of "Guard"* the
point is higher than the wrist; to give point, the latter
is lowered smartly, and the wrist is advanced at the
same instant. This double motion causes the point to
describe very nearly a cycloïd, the curvature of which
is analogous to, but in the inverse direction to that
of our blades, approaching to the curve of the
yataghan (the sword of the foot-soldier in the East.
It is short, slightly curved : its cutting edge is concave). This shape (Fig. 34) is so well adapted to the
object in view, that in France, in duels with the sword,
those who wish to make use of the point particularly
hold the curved sword upside down, so that in the
position of "Guard" the edge is upwards; thus, to
gain the advantage of a curvature of blades, analogous
to that described by the point, the combatant sacrifices
the use of the edge and the defensive effect of the hilt.
It is further to be observed that in holding the sword
in any other way, the impulse resulting from the two
motions is so directed, that the point penetrates as
though its angle were nearly double.

If a swordsman place himself at the end of a plastered wall, so as to be able to see along it lengthwise;
that the point of his sword be held resting against
the plaster; and that in this position points be given
agreeably to the principles of the sword-exercise on
horseback and on foot, leaving each time the curved
track of the sword point on the wall—we shall find
that the former points are nearly in a straight line,
and that the latter are curved to about the same

* Vide note, p. 49.

extent as our swords, but in the inverse direction,
like the yataghan.

There are two ways of stabbing with a poignard
—either holding it like a short sword, or having the
blade next the little finger. Leaving the marks on
the plastered wall as above, we shall find that in the
first case the tracks are straight, and that in the
last they are curved. Poignards should be straight
in the first case (Figs. 35 and 36), and curved in the
second (Fig. 37), as is actually the case. Experiment and theory have doubtless pointed out to nations,
according to their manner of using them, the most
suitable shape for poignards.

In the mechanical arts, in nature, in the arms of
various nations, that the point should have capacity
for penetration, we find that the penetrative instrument is either straight or curved in form, according
as the blow made therewith is in a straight or in a
curved line; in the latter case the curvature closely
approaches the curve described by the point.

Such is the reason and explanation: 1st. Of the
straight form of pikes, sounding-leads, common nails,
punches, &c.; of the offensive arms, of the sword- and
saw-fishes, of the stings of bees, of ancient swords
intended to pierce through armour, of arrows, javelins,
spears, and daggers of the Indians, Japanese, and
Spaniards, all of which strike like the short-sword; of
the bayonet, &c. 2nd. Of the *curved* form of pick-
axes, mattocks, horse-shoe nails, &c.; of the tusks and
claws of the carnivora; of the long, fragile, and venomous teeth of certain serpents; of the tail of the scor-

pion; of the bill of birds of prey; of the tusks of the wild board and elephant; of the horn of the rhinoceros; of the Turkish poignard, which strikes in the line of curvature traced by the rotation of the wrist round the shoulders; of the yataghan, the point of which acts like the tusks of an elephant, by a motion of translation combined with one of rotation.

Our arms it would appear, then, should follow the same rule. In the usual stroke with the point, the point of the sword in the cavalry describes a straight line, and in the infantry a curved one; the blades, consequently, should be straight for cavalry, and curved for infantry, but in the opposite direction to the existing curvature.

It is evident, that if the arms and tools abovementioned as being curved, were curved in the opposite direction, the difficulty of penetration would be much increased. This is the case with our infantry swords.

7. The wrist gives motion to the sword, and that it should do so without loss of power, it should thrust in the direction of the centre of gravity; or in other words, in a line, which starting from the middle of the origin of the hilt, passes through the centre of gravity of the sword.

In thrusting, that the motion communicated to the sword should react without loss on the point, the stroke must be made in the direction of the line joining the centre of gravity and the point of the sword.

That the pressure by the wrist on the point at the moment of impact, should have its effect without loss, it should be made, in a line starting from the centre of the origin of the hilt and passing through the point.

That the wrist should communicate the maximum of velocity to the sword, that this velocity should be transmitted at its best to the points, and that the pressure of the wrist on the point at the moment of impact be as great as possible, it is requisite that these three lines of impulses should coincide, that is to say, that *the centre of gravity should be situate on the line joining the centre of the origin of the hilt and the point.* This is the case exactly in the yataghan, and very nearly so in the straight sword. The lines of impulse form with each other angles, greater as the curvature of the sword increases; this is the reason why curved swords are but little adapted for thrusting.

In the blade of a straight sword the centre of gravity is nearer the back than the edge; but the hilt being situated more towards the edge than the back, the centre of gravity of the sword is consequently nearer the edge than the back. In order that there should be but one line of action of the three forces of impulse on the points, the centre of gravity should be placed at the edge; at the back its situation is the least favourable to the decomposition of the forces.

That the point should best resist the shock sustained in cutting, it should be at the back of the blade.

Finally, that the blade in the act of penetration should have the least possible tendency to deviate from the original direction, the point should be situated on the line of the centres of gravity of the cross

sections of the blade; that is to say, it should be in
the centre, if at the end of the blade, the thickness of
metal be systematical; and nearer the back, if the
latter be more weighted with metal.

Combining these three considerations, the position
of the point should be, it would appear, in the line of
the centre in the straight sword.

The apex should form an angle of forty degrees, as
is usually the case, and this angle should be bisected
by the line of impulse, taking as such a line starting
from the point and abutting at one third way, across
the origin of the grip, measuring from the edge side
thereof; thus, this line will be situated between the
**two directions of impulse which lie very close to each
other.**

With this sword in a thrust, the point will open a
passage for itself, its edges cutting under an angle of
twenty degrees on each side of the line of impulse of
the centre of gravity and of the hilt.

In the straight sword having the points at the back,
the line of impulse passes through the angle at the
apex, but does not bisect it; there is consequently less
force and greater difficulty of penetration.

In the yataghan there are two directions of stroke
to be considered (Fig. 34.), and the point may vary in
position from the middle to the back according to the
curvature of the blade. The curve thrust is more
certain in its effect with the point in the centre, and
in the straight thrust in having it at the back. Generally speaking, it is well placed at one third of the
breadth from the back.

In our light-cavalry sword (Fig. 45.), the **line of impulse** is exterior to the angle of the point and make with the angle of the back, an angle of about ten degrees. Its point forms an angle of forty degrees; it penetrates consequently, as though that angle amounted to fifty degrees. Besides, the velocity of the blade transmitted to the point is decomposed " to loss." The point would penetrate much better if it were situated in the medial line of the blade, having its angle bisected by the line which goes from the apex to one third way across the origin of the blade, measuring from the edge side. If the cavalry sword is to retain its present curvature, it is clearly desirable that the point should be thus situated.

With the Mameluke sabre, used in thrusting, we shall observe that the line of impulse which passes through the point and grip forms an angle of twenty-five degrees with the back of the point; the back and cutting edge of the point make an angle of forty degrees; penetration takes place by an edge inclined to the line of impulse at an angle of sixty-five degrees. The thrust would tend towards making a large wound, similar to that made by a cut; there would be a great loss in the communication of the velocity of the wrist to the centre of gravity and thence to the point. This weapon, moreover, is intended exclusively for cutting.

Several patterns of straight swords, with the point in the centre, have the two flanks which form it in straight lines, making an obtuse angle and joining the back and edge in a manner which leaves a projecting angle; this is a mistake. The point should be in the

centre, its angle about forty degrees, and its sides
should slope away to the back and edge in cutting
curves.

It is to be remarked, that practice in thrusting
makes these different values of swords to be well
appreciated by the swordsman, as well as the amount
of actual useful impulse they can receive and the
proper situation of the points. The difference of
effect is so sensible, that it is taken cognizance of by
the private soldiers. Thus in the regiments of heavy
cavalry in France there are various patterns of swords
(Fig. 52.); that of the year xiii is straight, it has three
grooves on the flats, and the point is at the back
(Fig. 53.); that of 1816 is straight, the point is in the
centre and it slopes off well and gradually into the
back and edge. The point in both cases has the
same angles, but that of the latter ought evidently to
penetrate better than the former; and herein experiment and theory agree; if the effects produced in
the heads and posts exercise in the riding-school be
examined, we shall find that the troopers armed with
the first-described swords rarely pierce the heads in
thrusting, that almost all the men who succeed in so
doing are armed with swords of the latter pattern, and
that frequently a sharp trooper, if his own sword be of
the former pattern, will borrow one of the latter just
before starting.

During the time of the Empire, in some corps the
pattern was altered by forming a sharp point to the
straight sword of the year xiii, with the idea of increasing its power of penetration: this would have

been more judiciously effected had the point been made in the centre.*

8. Let us now examine, agreeably to what precedes, the penetrative faculty of each of the following weapons: the yataghan, the straight forward, the present cavalry sword, and the lance.

First—In the yataghan (Fig. 34) the communication of force from the wrist to the centre gravity of the weapon, from the grip to the point, and from the centre of gravity of the weapon to the point, is very well effected. These three lines coincide. The line of impulse bisects the point; the shape of the blade is such that the size of its wound is a minimum, and it has the least possible tendency to deviate in direction in the curved thrust; but it is faulty in this respect in the straight thrust. It is the best weapon existing for the curved thrust. For the straight thrust it is inferior to the straight sword, but far superior to the curved sword with a curved edge.

Second—The heavy-cavalry sword (Fig. 58) of the pattern of 1816, is straight, with the points in the centre. The communication of force is well effected; the angle at the point is bisected by the line of impulse in the straight thrust, but the point acts under an angle almost double in the curved thrust. The shape of the blade is but little adapted for the curved thrust, both as to the width and depth of the wound inflicted by it, but it is the best pattern in these respects for the straight thrust.

* This is actually now the case in the corps of the French army armed with this sword. T.

Third—The sword of the year xiii (Fig. 52) is less adapted for thrusting than the preceding, because the point is situated at the back of the blade.

Fourth—The present cavalry sword (Fig. 44) does not communicate the force so well; it penetrates in the straight thrust under an angle greater than the actual angle of the point; it inflicts a wider and less deep wound, in consequence of its curvature and deviation. These defects are marked in the curved thrust.

Fifth—The greater the curvature of swords having a curved edge, the less are they calculated for pointing, **in consequence of the proportionate increase of the** preceding defects.

Thus, in all respects, as a weapon **to be used in** straight thrusting, the straight sword is the best; **but** for curved thrusting the yataghan is to be preferred to the straight sword, which again is preferable to the curved sword; for all thrusts, whether straight or curved. The straight sword and the yataghan, are preferable to the curved patterns, having a curved edge; the latter deteriorate in proportion to the increase of curvature.

Sixth—The lance penetrates by velocity, and not by pressure; the whole impulse reacts on the point without loss. The latter moves in a straight line; the weapon is straight, and is altogether constructed under the best possible condition for inflicting a wound of maximum depth.

9. The general shape of a weapon being judicious—granting that the wound made by a thrust should be of the same dimensions as the part of the blade which

penetrates, and that it should be as deep as possible, with the smallest possible opening—it follows that the cross-section of the blade, at that part which penetrates, should have a small area, sufficient to give the blade the requisite rigidity and strength. It is seldom necessary that the point should penetrate deeper than one decimetre (four inches).*

10. The rules relative to the grip and hilt seem to me to be identical for both thrusting and cutting.

11. The straight sword should be light and rigid: if it has capacity for cutting, that quality may be of service in its use. This weapon having little weight towards the point, and being slight generally, cannot penetrate with facility and certainty otherwise than by the direct impulse of the wrist. For this reason the blade should be straight. By giving it a shape analogous to that of some swords, which have broad and fluted backs, we should obtain a light stiff sword, capable of cutting. The hilt should be light, excepting at the pummel. I have had swords of this pattern made up; they appear to effect the object of thrusting well, and have a slight capacity for cutting.

12. Rigidity and lightness are particularly essential in the bayonet; the wide-fluted back is then judicious, and by means of this, moreover, a cutting-edge may

* I was informed by Major J. Crovone, of the Sardinian staff corps, that the Piedmontese Lancers, in the campaign against the Austrians in 1848-49, found at times great difficulty in withdrawing their lance from the body of a wounded enemy. To obviate this, at the bottom of the blade a round knob was welded on, which prevented penetration beyond the requisite depth. For the same purpose the Arabs have a small bunch of ostrich feathers in the like situation. The present regular Turkish Cavalry are armed with lances similar to the Sardinian pattern. T.

be obtained. I have had a bayonet made up with this idea; the back is turned towards the muzzle, and the cutting edge outwards. The bow, which joins the blade to the socket, is open, giving it advantageous rigidity; by grasping the weapon by the socket and putting the index finger through the bow, both point and edge may be used. The bayonet may thus become an arm capable of being used in the hand, having a certain value. The socket remains unaltered. The opening in the bow gives that part greater strength, which in the present bayonet frequently breaks.

CHAPTER II.

RECAPITULATION OF THE PRINCIPLES INVOLVED IN ARMS USED FOR THRUSTING.

First—Lightness in the weapon is not so necessary in thrusting as in cutting.

Second—The blade should be stiff, which involves thickness of metal; it should be light, so as to be suitable for cutting. To reconcile these conditions, the back may be thick and fluted.

Third—The angle of the point should be as acute as possible, and the line of impulse should bisect it.

Fourth—There are two sorts of thrusts, differing widely from each other : that in which the point moves in a straight line, and that in which it describes a curve.

Fifth—The general form of the blade should be analogous to that of the line described in the thrust.

Sixth—Cavalry swords should be straight, and

infantry swords should be somewhat curved, with the cutting edge at the concavity of the blade.

Seventh—The point of the sword should be on the medial line of the width of the blade; its angle should be bisected by the line running from the apex to one-third of the width of the blade near the grip, measuring from the edge.

In the yataghan the point, generally speaking, should be at one-third of the width from the back.

In our present cavalry sword, the point should be on the medial line of the width of the blade. The line of impulse will bisect the angle at the apex, as is the case in the straight sword.

In all cases the point should slope away to the back and edge by curved lines.

Eighth—As a weapon to be used in thrusting, the straight sword is the best in every respect for the straight thrust; the yataghan for the curved thrust; both are superior in either case to the curved-pattern swords with curved edge; the latter are the less adapted for both purposes, in proportion to the amount of curvation.

Ninth—The last decimetre (four inches) of the blade near the point should, as much as possible, be peculiarly calculated for thrusting, and to this end, should have its cross section of as small an arm as possible.

Tenth—The grip and hilt are identical in using both point and edge.

Eleventh—The straight sword should have a straight, rigid, slight blade, having as much power of cutting as possible. These conditions may be fulfilled, by adopt-

ing a shape analogous to that of the sword with thick
fluted back, and a light hilt weighted at the pummel.

Twelfth—This same form may be given to the
bayonet, which can be made a weapon to be used in
the hand, aving a certain value, and this without
altering the socket.

PART III.

ON ARMS USED BOTH FOR CUTTING AND THRUSTING.

—————

CHAPTER I.

DISCUSSION OF THE PRINCIPLES INVOLVED IN ARMS USED FOR BOTH CUTTING AND THRUSTING.

IT is difficult for a weapon to unite both qualities in the highest degree. Thus we see in the East horsemen cut with the Mameluke sabre, which is for the purpose the most perfect pattern, and only point with the lance or straight sword.* It is necessary that we should be able with the same sword, first to thrust well, and then to cut tolerably. Let us examine what this leads to in different arms :

1. For cavalry the blade should be straight. The effective use of the cutting edge necessitates weight at the last four decimetres (sixteen inches) of the blade, while that of the point requires a small volume at the last decimetre (four inches). To reconcile these two objects, the end of the blade might be made as though for pointing only, and then slope away up to the part

---

* The East, for a Frenchman, means European and Asiatic Turkey. If so, the author is not quite correct in his statement, as the greater part of the Turkish Bashi-bazouks and other irregular horsemen are armed with the yataghan. The exceptions being the leaders and rich men, who could afford to buy a scimetar. T.

of rest of the blade intended for cutting; this may be effected in two ways:

First—The hollow back of the blade may taper to this point, stopping short within a half-decimetre (two inches) of the latter, and being there replaced by a cutting-edge running up to the point.

Second—The fluted back of the blade may stop short at a decimetre and a-half (six inches) from the point, whence the end of the blade would form a double cutting-edge, as is usually the case, but with this difference, that the metal should be thicker, its maximum thickness being in the centre of the width without forming a ridge, and that the swell should abut at the point.

The remainder of the blade would be, in either case, like that described for cutting, as light as possible about the origin of the blade and at the hilt, with a rather heavy pummel. Swords of this pattern would thrust and cut better than those of the present pattern.

I have had swords made up of both fashions. I used them for nine years in Africa and found them efficient; but the second method of shaping the end of the blade was the best.

In the German broad-sword exercise they have a system of cutting which is sometimes used; it is of great power and unknown in France. This is done by striking with the back of the blade by a peculiar motion of the wrist, which adds much to the rapidity of the stroke. It is more especially applicable to cutting to the left-hand. It would be well to adopt this cut, as the weak side of the trooper is his left rear;

it is here that the pursuer should attack the pursued. This object seems sure to settle the question in favour of giving the preference to the sword having a cutting edge of a decimetre and a-half (six inches) in length at the back near the point, rather than to that of which the fluted back reaches close up to the point.

2. Cavalry swords shaped like a yataghan have one peculiar advantage; it is this, that by means of a slight movement of rotation of the hand, the cut may become a thrust moving with the velocity usual in the act of cutting, and the stroke would be consequently very dangerous. I have had three specimens made: 1st, with a fluted back: 2nd, like our present sword reversed: and 3rd, with a ridge in the centre and two cutting-edges. I have tried them: they answer for combat on foot better than the straight sword and *à fortiori* than the curved. On horseback the straight sword is to be preferred, but the yataghan-shaped sword is much better than the present sword.

3. For the infantry officer's sword, the yataghan-shaped blade should have the same thickness as those of the present sword, but be curved in the opposite direction; the point should be at one-third of the width from the back, and be bisected by the line of impulse.

The back may be fluted to give the blade rigidity, and the remainder of the blade be analogous to what has been described for the cavalry sword.

The blade being short and less likely to bend than that of the cavalry, rigidity might likewise be obtained by giving a ridge to each flat of the blade, near the

back, thus forming an obtuse edge. To the faculty of
pointing well, and of cutting well and powerfully with
a broad surface, this blade would have that of striking
with the blunt edge of the back, so as to inflict a slight
wound, an advantage which might be of service under
many circumstances out of the domain of actual warfare. This gradation of effect would render it preferable, for instance, as the armament of policemen to
the straight sword, which can only wound by a thrust,
that is to say, very dangerously.

I have had swords made up of these three patterns;
the second of the three seems to me to be preferable.

I will add, that if two men on foot cross swords, the
one with a sword of the present infantry pattern, the
other with one of the yataghan shape, each of the two
adversaries will feel the superiority of the latter weapon:
it will be quite sufficient to see them to account for
this.

4. The private's sword in the infantry, termed
" Briquet,"* may be modified as follows : it should be
made yataghan shape, the blade should be very wide
at the cutting part and have a point well calculated for
penetration, while the remainder of it should be
lightened by diminishing the width ; the back should
be ground to an edge for cutting wood. The greatest
thickness of metal should be at two-thirds of the width
of the blade from the edge, the point should be on the
line of ridge of the swell ; a brass grip should close
the mouth of the scabbard ; it should be narrow in the

---

* *Vide* note, page 88.

direction of the width of the blade. The bearing of the little finger should be wide and smooth. This sword would cut and thrust well; as a weapon its point and concave cutting edges would both be serviceable, while as a tool its convex edges would be found useful. I have had swords of this pattern made, and have tried them, and they appear to realise the advantages presumed by theory.

5. The present sabre-poignard would seem to be susceptible of improvement by being modified to the yataghan shape. One of the cutting edges would have the advantages possessed by the curved hatchet, the other those of a bill-hook. The point too would act better: it should be situated at one-third of the width from the convex edge. I have tried swords of this pattern; they seem to be handy.

6. Boarding cutlasses in the navy are not usually worn on the person; they are only used in actual combat, and immediately afterwards they are returned to the arm-rack. They do not require to be made of a portable form, like cavalry and infantry swords. They should be well adapted for thrusting in combat on foot, this would involve the yataghan shape, and in addition to this, they should cut as well as possible. The edge might be serrated at angles of forty-five, giving the weapon the flame-shape, while the medial lines form the yataghan curve. The undulations should commence at a distance of one decimetre (four inches) from the point and extend down the blade for three decimetres (twelve inches); the back should likewise be ground to a cutting edge; the greatest thickness of

metal at every part of the blade should be at two-thirds of the width from the concave edge, the point should hold the same position. The sword would thus retain its power of cutting, while its capacity for thrusting would be much increased.

7. Mounted men of all arms should be able both to cut and thrust. With men of all sizes, the method of using the sword is the same: it would seem, then, that their swords **should** all be of the same shape, but varying in dimensions according to the size of the soldier: thus there might be three sizes of swords, identical in shape, for mounted corps.

It is to be remarked that at the present moment there are four sizes in the service: the horse-artillery sword, the old "bancal," and the two new patterns. They are distributed of the different patterns by corps; so that we can imagine a certain light-dragoon, who happens to be bigger than the ordinary men of cuirassiers, being armed with a smaller sword than his mailed comrade; while a trumpeter or *enfant de troupe* of cuirassiers, who has the cut of an hussar, wears the largest sword in the service. It would seem advisable that in each corps, there should be swords of two sizes identical in shape, so that in every arm of the service the men should have weapons suitable to their size and strength.

8. To be able to make use of both point and edge, it seems to be indispensably requisite that the soldier should practise pointing, and more particularly cutting *in reality.* "Going through the motions" is not sufficient. It would seem a matter of no great difficulty for each

regiment to have a few swords kept specially for this purpose. By applying theoretic principles in cutting through bundles of straw, branches of trees, &c., the soldier would acquire that which practice alone can give in the use of the sword. He would use his weapon to better advantage and would have more confidence in it.

CHAPTER II.

RECAPITULATION OF THE PRINCIPLES INVOLVED IN ARMS USED FOR BOTH CUTTING AND THRUSTING.

First—For cavalry, the sword should be straight, rigid, light, and well balanced; have power of cutting, and long sharp edge; the point placed in medial line of the blade and bisected by the line running from thence to one-third of the width of the grip at its origin measured from the edge; the sides of the angle of the point should slope away in curved lines into the back and edge. The part of the blade near the point should be thickest in the centre and be without ridges; the last decimetre (four inches) should be shaped specially for pointing. The hilt and grip should be as described above.

Yataghan-shaped swords are less adapted for cavalry than the above, but more so than those of the present pattern.

Second—The infantry "briquet" should be made yataghan-shaped, wide at the cutting part, narrowing towards the point and origin; the back of the blade should have a cutting edge, and the point be situated at one-third distance from the back, the angle at the apex being bisected by the line of impulse.

Third—The sabre-poignard might advantageously be curved like the yataghan.

Fourth—Boarding cutlasses might, in addition to the yataghan curve for thrusting, have a flame-shaped portion of edge commencing at one decimetre (four inches) from the points, with the **view** of increasing its power of cutting.

Fifth—There should be three sizes of cavalry swords identical in shape, two of which should be found in each regiment.

Sixth—It would be advantageous that cavalry should practise thrusting and cutting *in reality*. They should practise too, the back stroke with the edge, to strike on the left side.

PART IV.

EXAMINATION OF THE PRINCIPAL ARMS IN EXISTENCE USED FOR CUTTING AND THRUSTING; AND RECAPITULATION.

CHAPTER I.

EXAMINATION OF THE PRINCIPAL ARMS IN EXISTENCE USED FOR CUTTING AND THRUSTING AMONG VARIOUS NATIONS.

First—Our present cavalry sword cuts and thrusts only moderately well, (Figs. 44, 45,) because it has little percussive force and little rigidity; and because its point, grip, and hilt, are injudiciously shaped.

Second — The "bancal" cuts better and thrusts worse than the preceding (Fig. 51); it is susceptible of improvement for both the one and the other; it should have greater percussive force without altering its weight or centre of gravity; the point should be situated on the medial line of the blade and be bisected by the line of impulse instead of being beyond it; finally, the grip and hilt should be corrected, both being defective.

Third—The heavy cavalry sword of the pattern of 1816 (Fig. 53), is ill-made at the hilt and grip, and it is faulty in not being sufficiently rigid, in that it hardly cuts at all, and, finally, in that the point, although

situate in the medial line, is not possessed of all the
faculty of penetration of which it is susceptible, owing
to the ridges which slope off into it, rendering both
the cutting edges very obtuse.

Fourth—The straight sword of the year xiii has a
portion of the above defects (Fig. 52); moreover, the
point loses much of its power of action, because it is at
the back of the blade, and slopes to the edge in very
nearly a straight line; so that in thrusting, this sword
strikes rather with a short cutting edge than with a
point.

Fifth — The infantry "briquet" might (Fig. 47)
with the same weight, cut and thrust much better,
because the grip, the shape of the flat of the blade,
the curvation and position of the point, are all faulty.
It is tolerably well adapted for cutting, but very ill for
thrusting.

Sixth—The infantry officer's sword has little percussive force, and cuts and points only moderately well;
its curvature, the position of the point grip, and hilt,
are all very faulty.

Seventh—The Mameluke sabre (Fig. 1) is perfect
for cutting. The British sword (Fig. 2), likewise,
cuts very well; these weapons are constructed on
different principles, but their application in each is
good: their defect is, that they are not adapted for
thrusting. The latter might be improved.

Eighth—The Turkish yataghan is an excellent
weapon for infantry; it thrusts and cuts well (Fig. 34).
The grip has no hilt, and consequently has no guard;
it likewise leaves the mouth of the sheath open, the

blade being wider near the point than at the origin; there is an empty space at the mouth of the sheath when the blade is home; this is closed either with a metallic cover attached by a chain, or with wax, the sheaths being luted on to the grip, both methods being unsatisfactory.

Ninth—The Kabyles manufacture in the Flessa range of mountains iron yataghans of an extravagant shape, rendering them much sought after by collectors of arms; they are very broad and tolerably thick at the cutting part; thus they are narrow up to the grip; this gives great percussive force, and the shape so far is rational; but they have further a very long, very thin, and very narrow point which bends without elasticity, injures the power of cutting, and is but little adapted for thrusting. If the points were shortened, this heavy and ill-balanced weapon would be well constructed as an iron yataghan; the defects of the material, as regards fineness of edge and rigidity of blade, would be compensated for by volume; it would stand half way between the steel yataghan and the mace.

Tenth—The blade should be in the direction of the fore-arm in the act of thrusting. To effect this, among certain nations, the Malays for instance, the grip is inclined to the blade at an angle of forty-five degrees; among others, the Indians to wit, the grip is at right angles to the blade in their straight swords and poignards. Our system seems better adapted for defence, and for the use both of point and edge.

Eleventh—Some hilts have grooves to fit the fingers;

E 3

this impedes the motion in the hand : moreover this
peculiarity is not met with in the arms of nations
famed for using them skilfully.

Twelfth—The pummel of certain Indian swords is
prolonged to a length of about fifteen centimetres,
(six inches) into an inclined metal shank protecting
the lower part of the arm and acting as a counterpoise.
This arrangement causes a loss of velocity in cutting,
by impeding the motion of the grip in the hand; it
would be well adapted for a sword intended to be used
in a duel on foot. I do not think it applicable to our
weapons meant for warfare.

Thirteenth—In certain Asiatic swords, the grip is
of wood; it is three decimetres (twelve inches) in
length, and has no bearing for the little fingers, the
reason of which may be that it is used double-handed,
although the blade is curved; or if used in the ordinary
manner, that it should act as a counterpoise and a
defence for the lower side of the arm. This peculiarity, though it has certain absolute advantages, does
not seem applicable to our arms, as it impedes the acts
of thrusting and cutting, besides being inconvenient in
carrying the weapon in a scabbard.

Fourteenth—The Roman swords were intended to
pierce armour with point and edge; the stuff not
having the hardness of steel, did not take a fine edge ;
in the later patterns they were straight, short, two-
edged, and heavy near the point to give percussive
force.

Fifteenth—The double-handed swords of the knights
of old were very long, broad, and tolerably thick ; they

had great percussive force, owing to their velocity and
volume, this being necessary to act with effect on
armour. With the same weight it would have been
quite possible to obtain a greater amount of effect by
the application of the principles above enunciated.

Sixteenth—Some two-handed swords were flame-
shaped. This arrangement, which enfeebles the
strength of the cutting-edge, seems more adapted for
cutting into bodies not protected by iron. I think it
is little applicable in the present day, because, among
other reasons, it involves a great width of scabbard.
It is only adapted for boarding-cutlasses.

Seventeenth—The serrated edge sword, in certain
straight blades, likewise has angles advantageous for
penetration; but as these points are weaker than a
continuous line, this arrangement is only found in very
**thick weapons, such as the broad thick blades of cer-
tain halberds.**

Eighteenth—In India there is a species of weapon
resembling a bill-hook. It is semi-circular, three
decimetres (twelve inches) in diameter, and is both
thick and broad in the blade; its handle is of metal,
four decimetres (sixteen inches) in length, and situated
in the line of the prolongation of the diameter which
connects the two extremities of the blade. Its blow
should be very powerful in consequence of the double
inclination of the edge. Some of these weapons have
a badly placed point at the part opposite the handle.
This arm appears to be susceptible of a great capacity
for cutting, if it were improved upon.

Nineteenth—Some savage nations who have no iron,

have a pointed weapon which strikes by a motion of rotation like our swords; it is a short club made of hard wood, having a tolerably sharp point placed perpendicularly to the length of the weapon near the centre of gravity, and projecting about fifteen centimetres (six inches). This arrangement causes the momentum of the club to act by a point instead of by a surface. The effect ought consequently to be greater as to depth.

Twentieth—On the breach at Constantine were found wooden clubs, the heads of which were garnished with iron spikes, a decimetre (four inches) in length. This weapon, like that which precedes, causes the club to act by a point instead of by a surface. The effect of the blow is very great, and it is difficult to parry; but it requires a great rotatory motion, and consequently leaves exposed the body of him who wields it; whereas in our system of using the point with our swords, the weapon itself is in a more defensive position, it admits of striking oftener in consequence of its lightness, and inflicts deeper wounds.

Twenty-first—Some battle-axes were shaped like a weathercock. The blade was flat and thin; it had two points intended to strike the object, distant from each other about two decimetres (eight inches), and had, further, four inclined cutting edges, so that the entire cutting edge was like the letter M. The intention of this weapon was to penetrate by the points and cut by the inclined lines of the M.

Twenty-second—In Asiatic countries there are, likewise, certain weapons like a Mameluke sabre recorded;

the cutting-edge is at the concave side, and the curvature of the blade is a complete half circle. The cutting-edge may act in two ways:—1st. By striking in the usual manner; this causes the blade to slide on the object from the point to the centre. 2nd. By drawing the weapon, as in using a sickle. It would appear that by using it in this manner astonishing effects are produced. 3rd. The motion of the blade in cutting may make a deep wound by striking with the point perpendicularly; or a less deep one, but having greater length, by striking obliquely. The weapon, in the latter case, acts like the wild boar's tusk. This sword is powerful as a weapon of offence, but it is feeble in a defensive point of view, in consequence of its shape; it is doubtless for this reason that its use is **very restricted.**

Twenty-third—Poignards, intended to be held with the blade next the thumb and to thrust like a short sword, are straight; some are narrow and straight, without cutting-edges; others act with a broad stiff blade. The grip is either in the direction of the blade, at an angle of forty-five degrees to it, or at right angles to it. Those intended to be held with the blade next the little finger are curved, and are more particularly intended for pointing; the grip is wider, as there is no motion inside the hand. In some of the latter species there is a channel ending near the points, which is filled with poison, like the fang of a viper. The poison is projected into the bottom of the wound by a peculiar mechanism.

There are, further, flame-shaped poignards. This

shape, the tendency of which is to widen the wound, is evidently faulty as a weapon specially intended for thrusting.

Twenty-fourth—The ancient Gauls made good use of an axe termed " Francisque ; " its blade was round, very sharp and wide, and it was thrown with great accuracy : its stroke must have been very powerful.

Twenty-fifth—In Asia there is a weapon of an analogous nature, and which, in well-skilled hands, is said to be very effective. It is a metallic quoit of about four decimetres (sixteen inches) in diameter, very sharp at the circumference, tolerably thin in metal, and having an empty space in the centre. It is thrown by giving it a sharp motion of rotation. It would seem that in consequence of the combination of weight, rectilineal velocity of the projectile, and circular velocity of the edge, its stroke is endowed with a great faculty of penetration.

CHAPTER II.

GENERAL RECAPITULATION OF THE PROPOSALS.

1. *The Hilt of the Sword.*—The hilt would be better made of steel than of brass ; the pummel should be somewhat weighted, the bearing of the little finger be wide and smooth ; nothing should be permitted to impede the motion of the little finger. The main branch should be stout, and as much out of the medial line as possible.

2. *The Grip.*—The grip should be smooth, narrow

in the direction of the width of the blade, especially at the points grasped by the index and fore-fingers.

3. *Distribution of Weight.*—The sword should be light, well balanced, and have percussive power. For this purpose the blade should be stout at the last four decimetres (sixteen inches) near the point; the pummel should be proportionately loaded; the rest of the blade should be as light as possible.

4. *The Edge.*—The edge should be formed by a long-sided sharp angle at the last four decimetres (sixteen inches). The stuff of which the blade is made ought to be such as to take a fine edge, and yet one that will resist a blow.

5. *Rigidity.*—For thrusting, the blade must be rigid. The shape which most rationally gives rigidity is that of a thick fluted back.

6. *Curvature.*—The general run of a blade intended to point should closely approach that of the line described by the point in the thrust; consequently, cavalry swords should be straight, and infantry swords should have a curve analogous to the present one reversed, the cutting-edge being at the concavity of the blade.

7. The point should form an angle of forty degrees at a maximum. This angle should be bisected by the line of impulse running from the apex to one-third of the breadth at the origin of the grip, measuring from the edge side. The point, in general, should be in the centre of the width of the blade in the straight sword, and at one-third of the width from the back in the yataghan-shaped sword.

In our present pattern swords, the point would be better placed in the centre than at the back, and being bisected by the line of impulse, instead of lying without that line, as is at present the case. It would appear to be advisable to alter our swords in this respect.

The sides of the point should slope away to the back and edge by curved lines. The last decimetre (four inches) of the blade ought to be formed solely for pointing. The blade at this part should have the smallest possible area of cross-section; there should be no ridge at the greatest thickness, which should be on a line running into the point.

8. *The end of the blade.*—The fluted back should stop short at fifteen centimetres from this point (six inches); then the blade, as is at present the case, should be smooth, and thicker than it is in the present pattern. It should have a swell in the centre without a ridge, the line of greatest thickness running into the point, with a cutting edge on each side.

9. *The Infantry "Briquet."*—The infantry "briquet" should be two-edged, and be shaped like a yataghan; it should be further wide at the cutting part and lightened along the rest of the blade. The grip should be formed agreeably to the principles above enunciated.

10. *The Infantry Officer's Sword.*—The infantry officer's sword should be yataghan-shaped; the back might be fluted up to within fifteen centimetres (six inches) from the point,* the rest of the blade agreeably to the principles enunciated.

---

* In the original it is "from the edge," but this is clearly a misprint.
       T.

11. *The Sword-poignard.* — The sword-poignard might be advantageously curved like the yataghan.

12. *The Boarding Cutlass.*—The boarding cutlass might have the yataghan shape, as advantageous in thrusting, be two-edged, and form one decimetre (four inches) from the point, be flame-shaped to increase its capacity for cutting.

13. *The Scabbard.*—The scabbard should have a piece of wood adapted to it, to preserve the fine edge from contact with the metal on the line of march, and especially in drawing or returning swords.

14. *The Sword-knot.* — The sword-knot should be supple, light, and be of silk or goats-hair, and have no large and heavy acorn at the end. It should be attached to the second branch of the hilt so as not to impede the little finger. The short-sword and the swords of infantry officers should be provided therewith.

15. The great billet of the sword-belt, and its ring and clasp on the scabbard, should be abolished.

16. *The Short Sword.*—The short sword might be fluted at the back up to twenty-seven millimetres (one inch) from the point, and have a cutting edge; the blade should be straight, and the hilt light, excepting at the pummel.

17. *The Bayonet.* — The bayonet might have a straight blade with fluted back, having a cutting edge on the side opposite the muzzle. The socket as at present; but the bow, being open, would be rigid and admit of the weapon being held in the hand both to cut and thrust.

18. *Sizes of Swords.*—There might be three sizes of cavalry swords identical in shape.

19. *Drills.*—The thumb should not be on the back of the grip in cutting. Some motions above alluded to in cutting should be modified, and others might be introduced. The men would have greater skill in using the sword if they were drilled at cutting and thrusting in reality.

THE END.

BRADBURY AND EVANS, PRINTERS, WHITEFRIARS.

MACHINERY.

57.

The text in 1 large vol. 8vo, and the plates, upwards of 70 in number, in an atlas folio volume, very neatly half-bound in morocco, price £2. 10s.

PRACTICAL ESSAYS ON MILL-WORK AND OTHER MACHINERY;

WITH EXAMPLES OF TOOLS OF MODERN INVENTION.

First published by ROBERT BUCHANAN, M.E.; afterwards improved and edited by THOMAS TREDGOLD, C.E.; and now re-edited, with the improvements of the present age,

By GEORGE RENNIE, F.R.S., C.E., &c., &c., &c.

USEFUL TO EXPERIMENTERS AND LECTURERS:

A SYSTEM OF APPARATUS

FOR THE

USE OF LECTURERS AND EXPERIMENTERS

IN

MECHANICAL PHILOSOPHY.

BY THE REV. ROBERT WILLIS, F.R.S.,

Jacksonian Professor of Natural and Experimental Philosophy in the University of Cambridge.

⁎ *For Contents of Work see other side.*

WITH THREE PLATES, CONTAINING FIFTY-ONE FIGURES.

Price 5s.

CONTENTS

Just published,

PAPERS

AND

PRACTICAL ILLUSTRATIONS

OF

PUBLIC WORKS,

OF RECENT CONSTRUCTION,

BOTH

BRITISH AND AMERICAN.

Supplementary to previous Publications.

CONTENTS:

Reviews, Communications, &c., American and Home Correspondence.

Fifty Engravings, price 25s.

JOHN WEALE.

1859.

ELEMENTS OF MECHANISM

ELUCIDATING

THE SCIENTIFIC PRINCIPLES

OF

THE PRACTICAL CONSTRUCTION OF MACHINES.

FOR THE

USE OF SCHOOLS AND STUDENTS IN MECHANICAL ENGINEERING.

WITH

NUMEROUS SPECIMENS OF MODERN MACHINES,

REMARKABLE FOR THEIR UTILITY AND INGENUITY.

BY T. BAKER, C.E.,

Author of "Railway Engineering," "Land and Engineering Surveying,"
"Mensuration," "Principles and Practice of Statics and Dynamics,"
"Integration of Differentials," &c. &c.

ILLUSTRATED BY TWO HUNDRED AND FORTY-THREE ENGRAVINGS.

Price 3s. 6d.

A

CATALOGUE OF WORKS

IN

ARCHITECTURE (CIVIL AND NAVAL),

AGRICULTURE, CHEMISTRY, ELECTRICITY,

ENGINEERING (CIVIL, MILITARY, & MECHANICAL),

MATHEMATICS, MECHANICS, METALLURGY,

ETC. ETC.

AND

Books in General & School Literature.

INCLUDING

MR. WEALE'S

SERIES OF RUDIMENTARY WORKS,

SERIES OF EDUCATIONAL WORKS, AND

SERIES OF GREEK AND LATIN CLASSICS.

PUBLISHED BY

LOCKWOOD AND CO.

STATIONERS' HALL COURT, LONDON, E.C.

1859.

A •

CATALOGUE OF WORKS

IN

ARCHITECTURE, AGRICULTURE, CHEMISTRY, ENGINEERING, MATHEMATICS, MECHANICS, METALLURGY, &c. &c.

PUBLISHED BY

LOCKWOOD & CO.,

STATIONERS' HALL COURT, E.C.

COMPLETE LIBRARY OF THE MILITARY SCIENCES.

Three vols., royal 8vo, upwards of 500 Engravings and Woodcuts, in extra cloth boards, and lettered, 4l. 10s.; or may be had in six separate parts, paper boards,

AIDE-MÉMOIRE TO THE MILITARY SCIENCES.

Framed from Contributions of Officers of the different Services, and edited by a Committee of the Corps of Royal Engineers. The work is now completed.

*** This work is admirably adapted as a present to the young Military Student, and should find a place on the shelves of every Regimental Library. It is recommended to the notice of Volunteer Rifle or Artillery Corps.

ALBAN ON THE HIGH PRESSURE ENGINE.

In 8vo, with 28 fine plates, 16s. 6d. cloth,

THE HIGH PRESSURE STEAM ENGINE.

An Exposition of its Comparative Merits, and an Essay towards an Improved System of Construction, adapted especially to secure Safety and Economy.

By DR. ERNST ALBAN,
Practical Machine Maker, Plau, Mecklenberg.

TRANSLATED FROM THE GERMAN, WITH NOTES,

By WM. POLE, C.E., F.R.A.S., Assoc. Inst. C.E.

BUCK ON OBLIQUE BRIDGES.

Second Edition, imperial 8vo, price 12s. cloth,

A PRACTICAL AND THEORETICAL ESSAY ON OBLIQUE BRIDGES,

With 13 large Folding Plates.

By GEORGE WATSON BUCK, M. Inst. C.E.

Second Edition, corrected by W. H. BARLOW, M. Inst. C.E.

CARR'S SYNOPSIS.

Second Edition, in 18mo, cloth, 5s.,

A SYNOPSIS OF PRACTICAL PHILOSOPHY.

ALPHABETICALLY ARRANGED,

containing a great variety of Theorems, Formulæ, and Tables, from the most accurate and recent authorities, in various branches of Mathematics and Natural Philosophy : to which are subjoined small Tables of Logarithms. Designed as a Manual for Travellers, Architects, Surveyors, Engineers, Students, Naval Officers, and other Scientific Men.

By the Rev. JOHN CARR, M.A.,
Late Fellow of Trinity College, Cambridge.

*** Sir John Macneill, C.E., a good authority, recommends this work to his pupils and friends.

NICHOLSON'S CARPENTER'S GUIDE and PYNE'S RULES on DRAWING.

A New Edition, with 74 plates, 4to, price 1l. 1s. cloth,

THE CARPENTER'S NEW GUIDE;

Or, Book of Lines for Carpenters. Comprising all the Elementary Principles essential for acquiring a knowledge of Carpentry, founded on the late PETER NICHOLSON'S standard work.

A New Edition, revised by ARTHUR ASHPITEL, Arch., F.S.A. ;

TOGETHER WITH PRACTICAL RULES ON DRAWING,

By GEORGE PYNE, Artist.

DEMPSEY'S PRACTICAL RAILWAY ENGINEER.

In One large Vol. 4to, price 2l. 12s. 6d. cloth,

THE PRACTICAL RAILWAY ENGINEER.

A Concise Description of the Engineering and Mechanical Operations and Structures which are combined in the Formation of Railways for Public Traffic; embracing an Account of the Principal Works executed in the Construction of Railways to the Present Time; with Facts, Figures, and Data, intended to assist the Civil Engineer in designing and executing the important Details required for those Great Public Works.

By G. DRYSDALE DEMPSEY, Civil Engineer.

Fourth Edition, revised and greatly extended.

With 71 double quarto plates, 72 woodcuts, and Portrait of GEORGE STEPHENSON.

LIST OF PLATES.

1 Cuttings	33 Creosoting, screw-piling, &c.	53 Watering apparatus—
2—4 Earthworks, excavating	34 Permanent way and rails	(A.) Tanks
5 Ditto, embanking	35 Ditto, chairs	54 Ditto, (B.) Details of pumps
6 Ditto, waggons	36 Ditto, fish-joints, &c.	55 Ditto, (C.) Details of engines
7 Drains under bridges	37 Ditto, fish-joint chairs	56 Ditto, (D.) Cranes
8 Brick and stone culverts	38—9 Ditto, cast-iron sleepers,&c.	57 Hoisting machinery
9 Paved crossings	40 Ditto, Stephenson's, Brunel's,	58 Ditto, details
10 Railway bridges, diagram	Heman's, Macneill's, and	59 Traversing platform
11—14 Bridges, brick and stone	Dockray's	60 Ditto, details
15—16 Ditto, iron	41 Ditto, Crossings	61 Station-roof at King's Cross
17—21 Ditto, timber	42 Ditto, ditto, details	62 Ditto, Liverpool
22 Centres for bridges	43 Ditto, spring-crossings, &c.	63 Ditto, Birmingham
23—27 "Pont de Monslou's"	44 Ditto, turn-table	64—6 Railway Carriages
28 "Pont du Cher"	45—6 Terminal station	66 Ditto, details
29 Suspension bridge	47—49 Stations	67—8 Railway Trucks and wheels
30 Box-girder bridge	50 Goods stations	69 Iron and covered waggons
31 Trestle bridge and Chepstow	51 Polygonal engine-house	70 Details of brakes
bridge	52 Engine-house	71 Wheels and details
32 Details of Chepstow bridge		72 Portrait

BARLOW ON THE STRENGTH OF MATERIALS.

With Nine Illustrations, 8vo, 18s. cloth,

TREATISE ON THE STRENGTH OF TIMBER,

CAST IRON, MALLEABLE IRON,

And other Materials; with Rules for Application in Architecture, the Construction of Suspension Bridges, Railways, &c.; and an Appendix on the Powers of Locomotive Engines on horizontal planes and gradients.

By PETER BARLOW, F.R.S.,

Hon. Member Inst. Civil Engineers, &c.

A New Edition by J. F. HEATHER, M.A., of the Royal Military Academy, Woolwich.

WITH AN ESSAY ON THE EFFECTS PRODUCED BY CAUSING WEIGHTS TO TRAVEL OVER ELASTIC BARS.

By Prof. WILLIS, of Cambridge.

————◆————

GREGORY'S MATHEMATICS, BY LAW.

Third Edition, in 8vo, with 13 Plates, very neatly half-bound in morocco, 1l. 1s.

MATHEMATICS FOR PRACTICAL MEN.

Being a Common Place Book of Pure and Mixed Mathematics, designed chiefly for the use of Civil Engineers, Architects, and Surveyors.

By OLINTHUS GREGORY, LL.D., F.R.A.S.

Third Edition, revised and enlarged by HENRY LAW, Civil Engineer.

CONTENTS.

PART I.—PURE MATHEMATICS.	PART II.—MIXED MATHEMATICS.
Chapter I. Arithmetic.—Chap. II. Algebra.—Chap. III. Geometry.—Chap. IV. Mensuration.—Chap. V. Trigonometry.—Chap. VI. Conic Sections.—Chap. VII. Properties of Curves.	Chapter I. Mechanics in General.—Chap. II. Statics.—Chap. III. Dynamics.—Chap. IV. Hydrostatics.—Chap. V. Hydrodynamics.—Chap. VI. Pneumatics.—Chap. VII. Mechanical agents.—Chap. VIII. Strength of Materials.—Appendix of Tables.

————◆————

A COMPLETE BODY OF HUSBANDRY, BY YOUATT.

Tenth Edition, much enlarged, with numerous Engravings, 8vo, price 12s. cloth, lettered, gilt back,

THE COMPLETE GRAZIER,

AND FARMER'S AND CATTLE BREEDER'S ASSISTANT.

A Compendium of Husbandry: containing full instructions on the breeding, rearing, general management, and medical treatment of every kind of stock, the management of the dairy, and the arrangement of the farm offices, &c.; description of the newest and best agricultural implements; directions for the culture and management of grass land, and of the various natural and artificial grasses, draining, irrigation, warping, manures, &c.

By WILLIAM YOUATT, Esq., V.S.,

Member of the Royal Agri. Soc. of England; Author of "The Horse," "Cattle," &c.

THE GREAT EASTERN AND IRON SHIPS IN GENERAL.

Second Edition, Atlas of Plates, with separate text, price 1l. 5s.,

ON IRON SHIP-BUILDING.

With Practical Examples and Details, in Twenty-four Plates, including three of the *Great Eastern*, together with Text containing Descriptions, Explanations, and General Remarks, for the use of Ship-owners and Ship-builders.

By JOHN GRANTHAM, C.E.,

Consulting Engineer and Naval Architect, Liverpool.

*** A work on the construction and build of Ships, by the application of Iron, has become now of the utmost importance, not only to Naval Architects, but to Engineers and Ship-owners. The present Work has been prepared, and the subjects drawn, in elevation, plan, and detail, to a scale useful for immediate practice, in a folio size, with figured dimensions, and a small Volume of text (which may be had separately, price 2s. 6d.)

DESCRIPTION OF PLATES.

1 Hollow and bar keels, stem and stern posts.
2 Side frames, floorings, and bilge pieces.
3 Floorings continued — keelsons, deck beams, gunwales, and stringers.
4 Gunwales continued — lower decks, and orlop beams.
5 Angle-iron, T iron, Z iron, bulb iron, as rolled for iron ship-building.
6 Rivets, shown in section, natural size, flush and lapped joints, with single and double riveting.
7 Plating, three plans, bulkheads, and modes of securing them.
8 Iron masts, with longitudinal and transverse sections.
9 Sliding keel, water-ballast, moulding the frames in iron ship-building, levelling-plates.
10 Longitudinal section, and half-breadth deck plans of large vessels, on a reduced scale.
11 Midship sections of three vessels of different sizes.
12 Large vessel, showing details—Fore-end in section, and end view with stern posts, crutches, deck beams, &c.
13 Large vessel, showing details—After-end in sec-

tion, with end view, stern frame for screw, and rudder.
14 Large vessel, showing details—Midship section, half-breadth.
15 Machines for punching and shearing plates and angle-iron, and for bending plates; rivet hearth.
16 Machines.—Garforth's riveting machine, drilling and counter sinking machine.
17 Air furnace for heating plates and angle-iron; various tools used in riveting and plating.
18 Gunwale, keel, and flooring; plan for sheathing iron ships with copper.
19 Illustrations of the magnetic condition of various iron ships.
20 Gray's floating compass and binnacle, with adjusting magnets.
21 Corroded iron bolt in frame of wooden ship; caulking joints of plates.
22 Great Eastern.—Longitudinal sections and breadth plans.
23 Great Eastern.—Midship section, with details.
24 Great Eastern.—Section in engine room, and paddle boxes.

READY RECKONER, INCLUDING FRACTIONAL PARTS OF A POUND WEIGHT.

24mo, 1s. 6d. cloth, or 2s. strongly bound in leather,

THE INSTANT RECKONER.

Showing the Value of any Quantity of Goods, including Fractional Parts of a Pound Weight, at any price from One Farthing to Twenty Shillings: with an Introduction, embracing copious Notes of Coins, Weights, Measures, and other Commercial and Useful Information; and an Appendix, containing Tables of Interest, Salaries, Commission, &c.

SIMMS ON LEVELLING.

Fourth Edition, with 7 plates and numerous woodcuts, 8vo, 8s. 6d., cloth.

A TREATISE ON THE PRINCIPLES AND PRACTICE OF LEVELLING,

Showing its application to purposes of Railway and Civil Engineering, in the Construction of Roads, with Mr. Telford's Rules for the same.

By FREDERICK W. SIMMS, F.G.S., M. Inst. C.E.

Fourth Edition, with the addition of Mr. Law's Practical Examples for setting out Railway Curves, and Mr. Trautwine's Field Practice of Laying out Circular Curves.

MOST USEFUL WORK FOR COUNTRY GENTLEMEN, FARMERS,
LAND AGENTS, &c.

New Edition, with Additions and Corrections, price 4s., strongly bound,

THE LAND VALUER'S BEST ASSISTANT.

Being Tables, on a very much improved Plan, for Calculating the Value of Estates.
To which are added, Tables for reducing Scotch, Irish, and Provincial Customary Acres
to Statute Measure; also, Tables of Square Measure, and of the various Dimensions of
an Acre in Perches and Yards, by which the Contents of any Plot of Ground may be
ascertained without the expense of a regular Survey, Miscellaneous Information on
English and Foreign Measures, Specific Gravities, &c.

By R. HUDSON, Civil Engineer.

"This new edition includes tables for ascertaining the value of leases for any term of years; and
for showing how to lay out plots of ground of
certain acres in forms, square, round, &c., with

valuable rules for ascertaining the probable worth
of standing timber to any amount; and is of incalculable value to the country gentleman and professional man."—*Farmer's Journal.*

INWOOD'S TABLES.

Seventeenth Edition. 12mo, cloth, 7s.,

TABLES FOR THE PURCHASING OF ESTATES,

Freehold, Copyhold, or Leasehold, Annuities, Advowsons, &c., and for the renewing
of leases held under cathedral churches, colleges, or other corporate bodies, for terms
of years certain, and for lives; also, for valuing reversionary estates, deferred
annuities, next presentations, &c., the Five Tables of compound interest, the Government Table of Annuities, and an extension of SMART'S Tables.

By WILLIAM INWOOD, Architect.

The Seventeenth Edition, with considerable additions, and new and valuable Tables of
Logarithms for the more difficult computations of the Interest of Money, Discount,
Annuities, &c., by Mons. FEDOR THOMAN, of the Société Crédit Mobilier, Paris.

NORMANDY'S COMMERCIAL HANDBOOK.

In post 8vo, illustrated with woodcuts, price 12s. 6d., handsomely bound in cloth,

THE

COMMERCIAL HANDBOOK OF CHEMICAL ANALYSIS;

Or, Practical Instructions for the Determination of the Intrinsic or Commercial Value
of Substances used in Manufactures, in Trades, and in the Arts.

By A. NORMANDY,

Author of "Practical Introduction to Rose's Chemistry," and Editor of Rose's
"Treatise of Chemical Analysis."

"We recommend this book to the careful perusal
of every one; it may be truly affirmed to be of uni-
versal interest, and we strongly recommend it to
our readers as a guide, alike indispensable to the
housewife as to the pharmaceutical practitioner."—
Medical Times.

"A truly practical work. To place the unscien-
tific person in a position to detect that which might
ruin him in character and fortune, the present work
will prove highly valuable. No one can peruse this
treatise without feeling a desire to acquire further

and deeper knowledge of the enticing science of
chemical analysis."—*Expositor.*

"The author has produced a volume of surpassing
interest, in which he describes the character and
properties of 400 different articles of commerce, the
substances by which they are too frequently adulte-
rated, and the means of their detection."—*Mining
Journal.*

"The very best work on the subject the English
press has yet produced."—*Mechanics' Magazine.*

NORMANDY'S CHEMICAL ATLAS AND DICTIONARIES.

The Atlas, oblong folio, cloth limp, 1l. 1s., the Dictionaries, post 8vo, 7s. 6d., cloth ; or, Atlas and Dictionaries together, 1l. 8s. cloth.

THE CHEMICAL ATLAS;

Or, Tables, showing at a glance the Operations of Qualitative Analysis. With Practical Observations, and Copious Indices of Tests and Re-actions ; accompanied by a Dictionary of Simple and of Compound Substances, indicating the Tests by which they may be identified; and a Dictionary of Re-agents, indicating their preparation for the Laboratory, the means of testing their purity, and their behaviour with Substances.

By A. NORMANDY,

Author of "The Commercial Handbook of Chemical Analysis," &c., &c., **and Editor** of H. Rose's "Treatise of Chemical Analysis."

"Tables such as these, like Maps and Charts, are more eloquent than the clearest prose statement. It is the most elaborate and perfect work of the kind that we are acquainted with."—*Mechanics' Magazine.*

"The work gives evidence of the author being perfect master of the task he has undertaken, and will no doubt occupy a place in the library of every chemical student and analyst."—*Mining Journal.*

"Several works on chemical analysis have for many years held a high position in the estimation of the scientific chemist. The work before us will be found in our opinion far more useful to the student of analysis, nay more, to the practitioner. The directions are more minute, and the number of cases introduced infinitely more varied. There is scarcely a possible case which the author has not provided for. From a careful examination we are able to say that any person possessed of a slight knowledge of chemical manipulation, may, by means of the Atlas and Dictionaries soon make himself a proficient analyst. Everyone who studies the Atlas must be impressed with the magnitude of the author's labour, and the vast extent to which he has economised the time and trouble of those who avail themselves of his friendly assistance."—*The Chemist.*

"'Normandy's Chemical Atlas' for comprehensiveness and completeness far surpasses anything of the kind hitherto published. I feel convinced that the student may with the aid of the Dictionaries, with which the Atlas is accompanied, successfully and alone undertake the examination of the most heterogeneous mixture, whether composed of organic or inorganic substances, or of both combined."—*Henry M. Noad, F.R.S., Lecturer on Chemistry at St. George's Hospital.*

By the same Author, crown 8vo, price 4s. 6d., cloth,

THE FARMER'S MANUAL OF AGRICULTURAL CHEMISTRY;

With Instructions respecting the Diseases of Cereals, and the Destruction of the Insects which are Injurious to those plants. Illustrated by numerous woodcuts.

"This work will be found of incalculable value to the Farmer. We have perused it with much interest, and have no hesitation in recommending it to the notice of every farmer, who will find it an excellent guide in all questions of Agricultural Chemistry."—*Agricultural Magazine.*

"By far the best attempt to supply a treatise of a limited kind on the chemical analysis of the materials with which the agriculturist is concerned ; the instructions are very satisfactory and are accompanied by illustrative figures of the necessary apparatus."—*Aberdeen Journal.*

SPOONER ON SHEEP.

Second Edition. 12mo., 5s. cloth.

THE HISTORY, STRUCTURE, ECONOMY, AND DISEASES OF THE SHEEP.

In Three Parts. Illustrated with fine Engravings from Drawings by W. Harvey, Esq.

By W. C. SPOONER, V.S.,

Member of the Council of the Royal College of Veterinary Surgeons ; Honorary Associate of the Veterinary Medical Association ; Author of "Treatise on the Influenza," and the "Structure, Diseases, &c., of the Foot and Leg of the Horse ;" Editor of White's "Cattle Medicine," and White's "Compendium of the Veterinary Art."

"The name of Mr. Spooner, who is a distinguished member of his Profession, is a sufficient guarantee for the accuracy and usefulness of its contents. Farmers' clubs ought to add this work to their libraries; and, as a work of reference, it ought to be in the possession of all Sheep Farmers."—*Gardeners' Chronicle.*

NOAD'S ELECTRICITY.

Fourth Edition, entirely re-written, in One Volume, illustrated by 500 woodcuts, 8vo, 1l. 4s. cloth,

A MANUAL OF ELECTRICITY.

Including Galvanism, Magnetism, Dia-magnetism, Electro-Dynamics, Magno-Electricity, and the Electric Telegraph.

By HENRY M. NOAD, Ph.D., F.C.S.,

Lecturer on Chemistry at St. George's Hospital.

Or in Two Parts :

Part I., ELECTRICITY and GALVANISM, 8vo, 16s. cloth.

Part II. MAGNETISM and the ELECTRIC TELEGRAPH, 8vo, 10s. 6d. cloth.

"This publication fully bears out its title of 'Manual.' It discusses in a satisfactory manner electricity, frictional and voltaic, thermo-electricity, and electro-physiology. To diffuse correct views of electrical science, to make known the laws by which this mysterious force is regulated, which is the intention of the author, is an important task."—*Athenæum.*

"Dr. Noad's Manual, in some departments of which he has had the counsel and assistance of Mr. Faraday, Sir William Snow Harris, Professor Tyndall, and others, giving an additional sanction and interest to his work, is more than ever worthy of being received with favour by students and men of science. The style in which it is written is very exact and clear."—*Literary Gazette.*

"Dr. Noad's 'Manual of Electricity' has for several years ranked as one of the best popular treatises on this subject. By an excellent method of arrangement, and a clear and agreeable style, he introduces the student to a sound elementary knowledge of every department of electrical science."—*Atlas.*

"This is a work of great merit, and is creditable to the scientific attainments and philosophical research of the author. Too much praise cannot be bestowed on the patient labour and unwearied application which were necessary to produce a work of such absorbing interest to the whole trading and commercial community."—*Educational Gazette.*

"On the subject of electricity, it is a service second only to discovery, when one competent for the task undertakes to sift and reconstruct the old materials, and to bring together and incorporate them with all that is important in the new. Such a service Dr. Noad has performed in his 'Manual of Electricity.'"—*Chambers' Journal.*

"As a work of reference, this 'Manual' is particularly valuable, as the author has carefully recorded not only his authorities, but, when necessary, the words in which the writers have detailed their experiments and opinions."—*Mechanics' Magazine.*

"Among the numerous writers on the attractive and fascinating subject of electricity, the author of the present volume has occupied our best attention. It is worthy of a place in the library of every public institution, and we have no doubt it will be deservedly patronised by the scientific community."—*Mining Journal.*

"The commendations already bestowed in the pages of the *Lancet* on former editions of this work are more than ever merited by the present. The accounts given of electricity and galvanism are not only complete in a scientific sense, but, which is a rarer thing, are popular and interesting."—*Lancet.*

TREDGOLD ON THE STRENGTH OF IRON, &c.

Fourth Edition, in Two Vols., 8vo, 1l. 4s., boards (either Volume may be had separately),

A PRACTICAL ESSAY ON THE STRENGTH OF CAST IRON AND OTHER METALS;

Intended for the assistance of Engineers, Iron-Masters, Millwrights, Architects, Founders, Smiths, and others engaged in the construction of machines, buildings, &c.; containing Practical Rules, Tables, and examples founded on a series of new experiments; with an extensive table of the properties of materials.

By THOMAS TREDGOLD, Mem. Inst. C.E.,

Author of "Elementary Principles of Carpentry," "History of the Steam Engine," &c. Illustrated by several engravings and woodcuts. Fourth Edition, much improved and enlarged. By EATON HODGKINSON, F.R.S.

HODGKINSON'S RESEARCHES ON IRON.

*** Vol. II. of the above consists of EXPERIMENTAL RESEARCHES on the STRENGTH and OTHER PROPERTIES of CAST IRON : with the development of new principles; calculations deduced from them; and inquiries applicable to rigid and tenacious bodies generally. By EATON HODGKINSON, F.R.S. With Plates and Diagrams, 8vo, 12s. boards.

ROGERS ON IRON METALLURGY.

With 20 carefully-prepared copper-plates. One Vol., 8vo, 1l. 5s., cloth.

AN ELEMENTARY TREATISE ON IRON METALLURGY,

Up to the Manufacture of Puddle Bars, built upon the Atomic System of Philosophy; the elements operated upon being estimated according to Dr. Wollaston's Hydrogen Scale of Equivalents; comprising suggestions relative to important Improvements in the Manufacture of both Iron and Steel, and the conduct of Extensive Iron Works; with Analytical Tables of Iron-making Materials.

By SAMUEL B. ROGERS, of Nant-y-Glo,

Inventor of Iron-Bottoms to Puddling-Furnaces, and of the present system of preparing Coke, in Double or Single Ovens.

"I do not hesitate to say that Mr. Rogers's work on Iron Metallurgy is, beyond comparison, the most complete combination of science and sound practice that has yet appeared on iron."—*David Mushet.*

"A volume which ought to be at hand in every Iron Works in the kingdom, and in the possession of every Ironmaster."—*Wolverhampton Chronicle.*

"Mr. Rogers does not come before the public as an untried theorist, for one of his inventions has been adopted generally throughout the Iron Manufactories of the world, and with immense advantage to Ironmasters."—*Bristol Times.*

"A remarkable book. Its author is, evidently, a man of practical experience, and of no mean scientific attainments, who has made the question on which he writes the business and study of his life."—*Staffordshire Advertiser.*

PYNE'S RULES FOR DRAWING.

In 4to, with 14 plates, in half cloth boards, 7s. 6d.

PRACTICAL RULES ON DRAWING,

FOR THE OPERATIVE BUILDER AND YOUNG STUDENT IN ARCHITECTURE.

By GEORGE PYNE,

Author of " A Rudimentary Treatise on Perspective for Beginners."

CONTENTS.

1 Practical Rules on Drawing.—Outlines.
2 Ditto.—the Grecian and Roman Orders.
3 Practical Rules on Drawing.—Perspective.

4 Practical Rules on Light and Shade.
5 Practical Rules on Colour.
&c. &c.

DOBSON and GARBETT'S STUDENT'S GUIDE.

In One Vol., 8vo, extra cloth, 9s.

THE STUDENT'S GUIDE

TO THE PRACTICE OF DESIGNING, MEASURING, AND VALUING ARTIFICERS' WORKS;

Containing directions for taking Dimensions, abstracting the same, and bringing the Quantities into Bill; with Tables of Constants, and copious memoranda for the Valuation of Labour and Materials in the respective trades of Bricklayer and Slater, Carpenter and Joiner, Sawyer, Stonemason, Plasterer, Smith and Ironmonger, Plumber, Painter and Glazier, Paper-hanger. With 43 plates and woodcuts. The Measuring, &c.,

Edited by EDWARD DOBSON, Architect and Surveyor.

Second Edition, with the Additions on Designs

By E. LACY GARBETT, Architect;

Together with Tables for Squaring and Cubing.

COTTAGES, VILLAS, AND COUNTRY HOUSES.

In 4to, 67 Plates, 1l. 1s. cloth,

DESIGNS AND EXAMPLES OF COTTAGES, VILLAS, AND COUNTRY HOUSES.

Being the Studies of Eminent Architects and Builders, consisting of plans, elevations, and perspective views; with approximate estimates of the cost of each.

RYDE'S TEXT BOOK FOR ARCHITECTS, ENGINEERS, SURVEYORS, &c.

In One large thick Vol. 8vo, with numerous engravings, 1l. 3s.

A GENERAL TEXT BOOK,

For the constant Use and Reference of Architects, Engineers, Surveyors, Solicitors, Auctioneers, Land Agents, and Stewards, in all their several and varied professional occupations; and for the assistance and guidance of country gentlemen and others engaged in the Transfer, Management, or Improvement of Landed Property, containing Theorems, Formulæ, Rules, and Tables in Geometry, Mensuration, and Trigonometry; Land Measuring, Surveying, and Levelling; Railway and Hydraulic Engineering; Timber Measuring; the Valuation of Artificers' Work, Estates, Leaseholds, Lifeholds, Annuities, Tillages, Farming Stock, and Tenant Right; the Assessment of Parishes, Railways, Gas and Water Works; the Law of Dilapidations and Nuisances, Appraisements and Auctions, Landlord and Tenant, Agreements, and Leases. Together with Examples of Villas and Country Houses.

By EDWARD RYDE, Civil Engineer and Land Surveyor,
Author of several Professional Works.

To which are added several Chapters on Agriculture and Landed Property,

By Professor DONALDSON,
Author of several Works on Agriculture.

CONTENTS.

WHEELER'S AUCTIONEERS', &c., ASSISTANT.

24mo, cloth boards, 2s. 6d.

THE APPRAISER, AUCTIONEER, AND HOUSE-AGENT'S POCKET ASSISTANT,

For the valuation, purchase, and the renewing of Leases, Annuities, Reversions, and of Property generally; prices for inventories, with a Guide to determine the value of the interiors, fittings, furniture, &c.

By JOHN WHEELER, Valuer.

TEMPLETON'S WORKSHOP COMPANION. SIXTH EDITION.

In 12mo, price 5s., bound and lettered,

THE OPERATIVE MECHANIC'S WORKSHOP COMPANION,

And THE SCIENTIFIC GENTLEMAN'S PRACTICAL ASSISTANT; comprising a great variety of the most useful Rules in Mechanical Science, divested of mathematical complexity; with numerous Tables of Practical Data and Calculated Results, for facilitating Mechanical and Commercial Transactions.

By W. TEMPLETON,
Author of "The Engineer's Common-Place Book," &c. &c.

Sixth edition, with eleven plates and the addition of Mechanical Tables for the use of Operative Smiths, Millwrights, Engineers, &c., and practical directions for the Smelting of Metallic Ores. To which also have been now added several useful and practical Rules in Hydraulics and Hydrodynamics, and an account of Dundas's Steam Hammer.

CONTENTS.

Geometry—Geometry applied to Mechanics—Decimal Arithmetic — Mensuration — Instrumental Arithmetic—Commercial Tables—Strength of Materials—Mechanic Powers—Continuous Circular | Motion—Friction—Properties of Water and Air—Steam Engine Boilers—Dundas's Steam Hammer—Logarithms.

THE BEST BUILDER'S PRICE BOOK.

Fourth Edition, in 12mo, cloth boards, lettered, 4s.,

WEALE'S BUILDER'S AND CONTRACTOR'S PRICE BOOK.

Published Annually. Containing the latest prices for work in all branches of the Building Trade, with items numbered for easy reference; and an Appendix of Tables, Notes, and Memoranda, arranged to afford detailed information commonly required in preparing Estimates, &c., for Builders and Contractors of Public Works.

WIGHTWICK'S HINTS.

With numerous Woodcuts. In 8vo, extra cloth, top edges gilt, 8s.,

HINTS TO YOUNG ARCHITECTS.

Comprising Advice to those who, while yet at school, are destined to the profession; to such as, having passed their pupilage, are about to travel; and to those who, having completed their education, are about to practise: together with a Model Specification; involving a great variety of instructive and suggestive matter, calculated to facilitate their practical operations; and to direct them in their conduct as the responsible agents of their employers; and as the rightful judges of a contractor's duty.

By GEORGE WIGHTWICK, Architect,
Author of "The Palace of Architecture," &c., &c.

CONTENTS.

Preliminary hints to young architects on the knowledge of drawing
On serving his time
On travelling
His plate on the door
Orders, plan-drawing
On his taste, study of interiors
Interior arrangements
Warming and Ventilating
Housebuilding, stabling
Cottages and villas
Model Specification

General Classes
Foundations
Well
Artificial Foundations
Brickwork
Rubble masonry with brick mingled
Stone-curbing
     "   Grecian or Italian only
     "   Gothic only
Miscellaneous
Slating
Tiling

Plaster and cement work
Carpenters' work
Joiners' work
Iron and metal work
Plumbers' work
Drainage
Well-digging
Artificial levels, concrete, foundations, piling and planking, paving, vaulting, bell-hanging, plumbing, and building generally.

TREDGOLD'S CARPENTRY. FOURTH EDITION.

In One large Vol. 4to., 2l. 2s., in extra cloth.

THE ELEMENTARY PRINCIPLES OF CARPENTRY;

A Treatise on the pressure and equilibrium of timber framing, the resistance of timber, and the construction of floors, arches, bridges, roofs, uniting iron and stone with timber, &c., with practical rules and examples; to which is added, an essay on the nature and properties of timber, including the method of seasoning, and the causes and prevention of decay, with descriptions of the kinds of wood used in building; also numerous tables of the scantlings of timber for different purposes, the specific gravities of materials, &c.

By THOMAS TREDGOLD, Civil Engineer.

Illustrated by fifty-three Engravings, a portrait of the author, and several Woodcuts. Fourth Edition, corrected and considerably enlarged. With an Appendix, containing specimens of various ancient and modern roofs.

Edited by PETER BARLOW, F.R.S.

CONTENTS OF PLATES.

HANDY BOOK FOR ACTUARIES, BANKERS, INSURANCE OFFICES, AND COMMERCIAL MEN IN GENERAL.

In 12mo, cloth, price 5s.

THEORY OF COMPOUND INTEREST AND ANNUITIES,

With TABLES of LOGARITHMS for the more difficult computations of Interest, Discount, Annuities, &c., in all their applications and uses for Mercantile and State purposes, with a full and elaborate introduction.

By FEDOR THOMAN, of the Société Crédit Mobilier, Paris.

"A very powerful work, and the Author has a very remarkable command of his subject."—*Professor A. de Morgan.*

"No banker, merchant, tradesman, or man of business ought to be without Mr. Thoman's truly 'handy-book.'"—*Review.*

"The author of this 'handy-book' deserves our thanks for his successful attempt to extend the use of logarithms."—*Insurance Gazette.*

"We recommend it to the notice of actuaries and accountants."—*Athenæum.*

WEALE'S ENGINEER'S POCKET BOOK.

With 8 copper plates, and numerous woodcuts, in roan tuck, 6s.

THE ENGINEER'S, ARCHITECT'S, AND CONTRACTOR'S POCKET BOOK.

Published annually. With DIARY of EVENTS and DATA connected with **Engineering**, Architecture, and the kindred Sciences, professionally and otherwise **revised.**

CONTENTS FOR 1860.

Alloys. Almanack
Ballasting. Barlow
Barrel Drains
Bessemer on the Manufacture of Iron and Steel
Boilers and Engines (Proportions of)
Boilers, Furnaces, and Chimneys
Calendar
Carpentry and Joinery
Cask and Malt Gauging
Castings, sundry for Sewers, Gasworks, &c.
Cast-iron Columns and Girders
Chairs for Railways
Chimneys, dimensions of
Circumference of Circles
Circular Arcs (Tables of)
Circle, Cylinder, Sphere, &c.
Coal Experiments; Economic Values of Coals
Coking (evaporative Powers of Coal, and Results of)
Columns, Posts, &c.
Copper Mines (Synopsis of) in Devon and Cornwall
Cornwall Pumping Engines
Current Coins
Du Buat
Earthwork
East London Waterworks
Eclipses
Elastic Properties of Steam
Ellipses, Cones, Frustrums, &c.
Ephemerides of the Planets
Fairbairn on the Mechanical Properties of Metals; on the tensile strength of Wrought Iron at various temperatures; Tubular Girder Bridges; Notes on Toughened Cast-iron; on the Resistance of Tubes to Collapse
Flooring
French and English Scales
Friction
Fuel on the American Railways and on English Railways
Gas Engineers' Calendar

Gauges (List of) and Weights of Galvanized Tinned Iron Sheets
Girders (Cast-iron)
Hawksley
Heat (Effects of)
High Water at London Bridge
Howard
Hydraulics
Hydrodynamics
Institution of Civil Engineers (List of Members of)
Institute of British Architects (List of Members of)
Iron Bar
Iron
—— Roofs
Knot Tables
Latitudes and Longitudes [&c.
Log. of Sines, Cosines, Tangents,
Marine Engines
Marine Screw Propulsion
Maristier
Masonry
Measuration (Epitome of)
Morin's Experiments on Friction; on Ropes
Natural Sines, &c.
Neville, on Retaining Walls
Notes to accompany the Abbreviated Table of Natural Sines
Peninsular and Oriental Steam Fleet
Probin [and Boilers
Proportions of Marine Engines
Proportional Sizes and Weights of Hexagon-heads and Nuts for Bolts
Pumping Water by Steam Power
Rails
Rennie (G.); Messrs. Rennie
Roofs
Ropes, Experiments of
Sewers
Sleepers for Railways
Smith's Sewer. Sound
Specific Gravity of Gases
Square, Rectangle, Cube, &c.
Square and Round Bar-Iron

Strength of Columns
Strength of Materials of Construction
Strength of Rolled T-Iron
Stone, Preservation of Stones
Tables of the Weight of Iron Castings for Timber Roofs
—— of the Properties of Different Kinds of Timber
—— of the Weights of Balls and Chains
—— of the Weight, Pressure, &c. of Materials, Cast-Iron, &c.
—— of Weights of Copper, Tin-Plates, Copper-Pipes, Cocks for Coppers, Leaden Pipes
—— for the Diameter of a Wheel of a Given Pitch
—— of the Weights of a Lineal Foot of Flat Bar-Iron, of a Superficial Foot of various Metals, &c.
—— of the Weight of a Lineal Foot of Cast-iron Pipes
—— of the Diameter of Solid or Cylinder of Cast-Iron, &c.
—— of the Diameter and Thickness of Metal of Hollow Columns of Cast-Iron
—— of Cast-Iron Stanchions
—— of Strength of Cast-Iron Bars
—— of the Values of Earthwork
—— of Weights and Measures
—— of Natural Sines
Teeth of Wheels
Telford's Memorandum Book
Thermometers
Timber for Carpentry and Joinery
Tredgold's Rule
Waterworks
Weights of Copper, Brass, Steel, Hoop-Iron, &c.
Weights and Measures
Weights of Rails
Wickstead
Woods

MR. WEALE'S SERIES OF

RUDIMENTARY, SCIENTIFIC, EDUCATIONAL, AND CLASSICAL WORKS,

At prices varying from 1s. to 2s. 6d.

Lists may be had on application to MESSRS. LOCKWOOD & Co.

✱✱✱ This excellent and extraordinarily cheap series of books, now comprising upwards of 150 different works, in almost every department of Science, Art, and Education, is strongly recommended to the notice of Mechanics' Institutions, Literary and Scientific Associations, Free Libraries, Colleges, Schools and Students generally, and also to Merchants, Shippers, &c.

CATALOGUE

OF

RUDIMENTARY, SCIENTIFIC, EDUCATIONAL, AND CLASSICAL WORKS

FOR

COLLEGES, HIGH AND ORDINARY SCHOOLS, AND SELF-INSTRUCTION.

ALSO FOR

MECHANICS' INSTITUTIONS, FREE LIBRARIES, &c., &c.

MR. WEALE'S

SERIES OF RUDIMENTARY WORKS

FOR THE USE OF BEGINNERS.

LONDON: JOHN WEALE, 59, HIGH HOLBORN.

WHOLESALE AGENTS, LOCKWOOD & CO., 7, STATIONERS' HALL COURT, E.C.

The several Series are amply illustrated, in demy 12mo., each neatly bound in cloth; and, for the convenience of purchasers, the subjects are published separately at the following prices:

1. CHEMISTRY, by Prof. Fownes, F.R.S., including Agricultural Chemistry, for the use of Farmers . . . . 1s.
2. NATURAL PHILOSOPHY, by Charles Tomlinson 1s
3. GEOLOGY, by Major-Gen. Portlock, F.R.S., &c. . . . 1s. 6d.
4, 5. MINERALOGY, with Mr. Dana's additions, 2 vols. in 1 . . . 2s.
6. MECHANICS, by Charles Tomlinson . . . . 1s.
7. ELECTRICITY, by Sir William Snow Harris, F.R.S. . . . 1s. 6d.

7.* ON GALVANISM; ANIMAL AND VOLTAIC ELECTRICITY; Treatise on the General Principles of Galvanic Science, by Sir W. Snow Harris, F.R.S. 1s. 6d.

8, 9, 10. MAGNETISM, Concise Exposition of, by the same, 3 vols. in 1. 3s. 6d.

11, 11* ELECTRIC TELEGRAPH, History of the, by E. Highton, C.E. . . 2s.

12. PNEUMATICS, by Charles Tomlinson . . . . 1s.

13, 14, 15, 15.* CIVIL ENGINEERING, by Henry Law, C.E., 3 vols.; and Supplement by G. R. Burnell, C.E., in 1 vol. . . . **4s. 6d.**

124. ON ROOFS FOR PUBLIC AND PRIVATE BUILDINGS, founded on Dr.
Robison's Work . . . . 1s. 6d.

124*. RECENTLY CONSTRUCTED IRON ROOFS, Atlas of plates . . 4s. 6d.

125. ON THE COMBUSTION OF COAL AND THE PREVENTION OF SMOKE,
Chemically and Practically Considered, by Chas. Wye Williams,
M.I.C.E. . . . . . . { The 2 vols. }
126. Illustrations to ditto . . . . . { in 1. } 3s.

127. RUDIMENTARY AND PRACTICAL INSTRUCTIONS IN THE ART OF ARCHI-
TECTURAL MODELLING, with Illustrations for the Practical Application of the Art, by J. A. Richardson, Arch. . . . 1s. 6d.

128. THE TEN BOOKS OF M. VITRUVIUS ON CIVIL, MILITARY, AND NAVAL
ARCHITECTURE,* translated by Joseph Gwilt, Arch., 2 vols. in 1, in
the press . . . . 2s. 6d.

129. ATLAS OF ILLUSTRATIVE PLATES TO DITTO, in 4to, with the Vignettes,
designed by Joseph Gandy, in the press . . . . 4s. 6d.

130. INTRODUCTION TO THE STUDY AND THE BEAUTY OF GRECIAN ARCHI-
TECTURE, by the Right Hon. the Earl of Aberdeen, &c., &c., &c.,
in the press . . . . 1s.

MR. WEALE'S

NEW SERIES OF EDUCATIONAL WORKS.

1, 2, 3, 4. CONSTITUTIONAL HISTORY OF ENGLAND, by W. D Hamilton . 4s.

5, 6. OUTLINES OF THE HISTORY OF GREECE, by the same, 2 vols. . 2s. 6d.

7, 8. OUTLINE OF THE HISTORY OF ROME, by the same, 2 vols. . 2s. 6d.

9, 10. CHRONOLOGY OF CIVIL AND ECCLESIASTICAL HISTORY, LITERA-
TURE, ART, AND CIVILISATION, from the earliest period to the
present, 2 vols. . . . . 2s. 6d.

11. GRAMMAR OF THE ENGLISH LANGUAGE, by Hyde Clarke, D.C.L. . 1s.

11*. HAND BOOK OF COMPARATIVE PHILOLOGY, by the same . . 1s.

12, 13. DICTIONARY OF THE ENGLISH LANGUAGE. A new Dictionary of
the English Tongue, as spoken and written, above 100,000 words,
or 50,000 more than in any existing work, by the same, 3 vols.
in 1 . . . . 3s. 6d.

14. GRAMMAR OF THE GREEK LANGUAGE, by H. C. Hamilton . . 1s.

15, 16. DICTIONARY OF THE GREEK AND ENGLISH LANGUAGES, by H. R.
Hamilton, 2 vols. in 1 . . . . 2s.

17, 18. ———————— ENGLISH AND GREEK LANGUAGES, by the
same, 2 vols. in 1 . . . . 2s.

19. GRAMMAR OF THE LATIN LANGUAGE, by the Rev. T. Goodwin, A.B. . 1s.

20, 21. DICTIONARY OF THE LATIN AND ENGLISH LANGUAGES, by the
same. Vol. I. . . . . 2s.

22, 23. ———————— ENGLISH AND LATIN LANGUAGES, by the
same. Vol. II. . . . . 1s. 6d.

24. GRAMMAR OF THE FRENCH LANGUAGE . . . . . . 1s.

---

* This work, translated by a scholar and an architect, was originally published at
36s. It bears the highest reputation, and being now for the first time issued in this
Series, the student and the scholar will receive it as a boon from the gifted translator.

25. DICTIONARY OF THE FRENCH AND ENGLISH LANGUAGES, by A. Elwes, Vol. I. . . . . 1s.

26. ———— ENGLISH AND FRENCH LANGUAGES, by the same. Vol II. . . . . 1s. 6d.

27. GRAMMAR OF THE ITALIAN LANGUAGE, by the same . . . 1s.

28, 29 DICTIONARY OF THE ITALIAN, ENGLISH, AND FRENCH LANGUAGES, by the same. Vol. I. . . . . 2s.

30, 31. ———— ENGLISH, ITALIAN, AND FRENCH LANGUAGES, by the same. Vol. II. . . . . 2s.

32, 33. ———— FRENCH, ITALIAN, AND ENGLISH LANGUAGES, by the same. Vol. III. . . . . 2s.

34. GRAMMAR OF THE SPANISH LANGUAGE, by the same . . . 1s.

35, 36, 37, 38 DICTIONARY OF THE SPANISH AND ENGLISH LANGUAGES, by the same, 4 vols. in 1 . . . . 4s.

39. GRAMMAR OF THE GERMAN LANGUAGE . . . . . . 1s.

40. CLASSICAL GERMAN READER, from the best authors . . . 1s.

41, 42, 43. DICTIONARIES OF THE ENGLISH, GERMAN, AND FRENCH LANGUAGES, by N. E. Hamilton, 3 vols., separately 1s. each . . 3s.

44, 45 DICTIONARY OF THE HEBREW AND ENGLISH LANGUAGES, containing the Biblical and Rabbinical words, 2 vols (together with the Grammar, which may be had separately for 1s.) by Dr. Bresslau, Hebrew Professor . . . . 7s.

46. ———— ENGLISH AND HEBREW LANGUAGES. Vol. III. to complete . . . . 3s.

47. FRENCH AND ENGLISH PHRASE BOOK . . . . . . 1s.

THE SERIES OF EDUCATIONAL WORKS

Are on sale in two kinds of binding ; the one for use in Colleges and Schools and the other for the Library.

HAMILTON'S OUTLINES OF THE HISTORY OF ENGLAND, 4 vols. in 1. strongly bound in cloth . . . . 5s.

———— Ditto, in half-morocco, gilt, marbled edges . . . 5s. 6d.

HISTORY OF GREECE, 2 vols. in 1, bound in cloth . . . 3s. 6d.

Ditto, in half-morocco, gilt, marbled edges . . . . 4s.

HISTORY OF ROME, 2 vols. in 1, bound in cloth . . . 3s. 6d.

Ditto, in half-morocco, gilt, marbled edges . . . . 4s.

CHRONOLOGY OF CIVIL AND ECCLESIASTICAL HISTORY, LITERATURE, ART, &c , 2 vols. in 1, bound in cloth . . . . . 3s. 6d.

———— Ditto, in half-morocco, gilt, and marbled edges . . 4s.

CLARKE'S DICTIONARY OF THE ENGLISH LANGUAGE, bound in cloth . 4s. 6d.

————, in half-morocco, gilt, marbled edges . . . . 5s.

————, bound with DR. CLARKE'S ENGLISH GRAMMAR in cloth . 5s. 6d.

————Ditto, in half-morocco, gilt, marbled edges . . . 6s.

HAMILTON'S GREEK AND ENGLISH and ENGLISH AND GREEK DICTIONARY,
   4 vols. in 1, bound in cloth . . . . 5s.

————————Ditto, in half-morocco, gilt, marbled edges . . . 5s. 6d.

————————Ditto, with the GREEK GRAMMAR, bound in cloth . . 6s.

————————Ditto, with Ditto, in half-morocco, gilt, marbled edges . 6s. 6d.

GOODWIN'S LATIN AND ENGLISH and ENGLISH AND LATIN DICTIONARY, 2
   vols. in 1, bound in cloth 4s. 6d

———— ———— Ditto, in half-morocco, gilt, marbled edges . . . . . 5s.

———————— Ditto, with the LATIN GRAMMAR, bound in cloth . . 5s. 6d.

———————— Ditto, with Ditto, in half-morocco, gilt, marbled edges . . 6s.

ELWES'S FRENCH AND ENGLISH and ENGLISH AND FRENCH DICTIONARY,
   2 vols. in 1, in cloth . . . . 3s. 6d.

———————— Ditto, in half-morocco, gilt, marbled edges . . . . 4s.

———————— Ditto, with the FRENCH GRAMMAR, bound in cloth . . 4s. 6d.

———————— Ditto, with Ditto, in half-morocco, gilt, marbled edges . . 5s.

FRENCH AND ENGLISH PHRASE BOOK, or Vocabulary of all Conversational
   Words, bound, to carry in the pocket . . . . . 1s 6d.

ELWES'S ITALIAN, ENGLISH, AND FRENCH,—ENGLISH, ITALIAN, AND
   FRENCH,—FRENCH, ITALIAN, AND ENGLISH DICTIONARY, 3 vols.
   in 1, bound in cloth . . . . 7s. 6d.

ELWES'S Ditto, in half-morocco, gilt, marbled edges . . . . 8s. 6d.

———————— Ditto, with the GRAMMAR, bound in cloth . . . . 8s. 6d.

———————— Ditto, with Ditto, in half-morocco, gilt, marbled edges . 9s.

———————— SPANISH AND ENGLISH and ENGLISH AND SPANISH DICTIONARY,
   4 vols. in 1, bound in cloth 5s

———————— Ditto, in half-morocco, gilt, marbled edges . . . . 5s. 6d.

———————— Ditto, with the GRAMMAR, bound in cloth . . . . . 6s.

———————— Ditto, with Ditto, in half morocco, gilt, marbled edges . 6s. 6d.

HAMILTON'S ENGLISH, GERMAN, AND FRENCH,—GERMAN, FRENCH, AND
   ENGLISH,—FRENCH, GERMAN, AND ENGLISH DICTIONARY, 3 vols.
   in 1, bound in cloth . . . . 4s.

———————— Ditto, in half-morocco, gilt, marbled edges . . . 4s. 6d.

———————— Ditto, with the GRAMMAR, bound in cloth . . . . 5s.

———————— Ditto, with Ditto, in half-morocco, gilt, marbled edges . 5s. 6d.

BRESSLAU'S HEBREW AND ENGLISH DICTIONARY, with the GRAMMAR, 3
   vols. bound in cloth . . . . 12s.

———————— Ditto, 3 vols., in half-morocco, gilt, marbled edges . . 14s.

Now in the course of Publication,

GREEK AND LATIN CLASSICS,

Price 1s. per Volume, (except in some instances, and those are 1s. 6d. or
2s. each), very neatly printed on good paper.

A Series of Volumes containing the principal Greek and Latin Authors,
accompanied by Explanatory Notes in English, principally selected from
the best and most recent German Commentators, and comprising all those

Works that are essential for the Scholar and the Pupil, and applicable for the Universities of Oxford, Cambridge, Edinburgh, Glasgow, Aberdeen, and Dublin,—the Colleges at Belfast, Cork, Galway, Winchester, and Eton, and the great Schools at Harrow, Rugby, &c.—also for Private Tuition and Instruction, and for the Library.

Those that are not priced are in the Press.

LATIN SERIES.

1 A new LATIN DELECTUS, Extracts from Classical Authors, with Vocabularies and Explanatory Notes . . . . . 1s.
2 CÆSAR'S COMMENTARIES on the GALLIC WAR; with Grammatical and Explanatory Notes in English, and a Geographical Index 2s.
3 CORNELIUS NEPOS; with English Notes, &c. . . . 1s.
4 VIRGIL. The Georgics, Bucolics, and doubtful Works: with English Notes . . . . . 1s.
5 VIRGIL'S ÆNEID (on the same plan as the preceding.) . . . 2s.
6 HORACE. Odes and Epodes; with English Notes, and Analysis and explanation of the metres . 1s.
7 HORACE. Satires and Epistles, with English Notes, &c. . 1s. 6d.
8 SALLUST. Conspiracy of Catiline, Jugurthine War . . 1s. 6d.

9 TERENCE. Andria and Heauton-timorumenos . . 1s. 6d.
10 TERENCE. Phormio, Adelphi and Hecyra . . . 1s. 6d.
11 CICERO. Orations against Catiline, for Sulla, for Archias, and for the Manilian Law.
12 CICERO. First and Second Philippics; Orations for Milo, for Marcellus, &c.
13 CICERO. De Officiis.
14 CICERO. De Amicitia, de Senectute, and Brutus . . 1s. 6d.
15 JUVENAL and PERSIUS. (The indelicate passages expunged).
16 LIVY. Books i to v. in 2 parts . 3s.
17 LIVY. Books xxi. and xxii. . 1s.
18 TACITUS. Agricola; Germania; and Annals, Book i.
19 Selections from TIBULLUS, OVID, PROPERTIUS, and LUCRETIUS.
20 Selections from SUETONIUS and the later Latin Writers. . 1s. 6d.

GREEK SERIES,
ON A SIMILAR PLAN TO THE LATIN SERIES.

1 INTRODUCTORY GREEK READER. On the same plan as the Latin Reader . . . . 1s.
2 XENOPHON. Anabasis, i. ii. iii. . 1s.
3 XENOPHON. Anabasis, iv. v. vi. vii. . . . . 1s.
4 LUCIAN. Select Dialogues . 1s.
5 HOMER. Iliad, i. to vi . 1s. 6d.
6 HOMER. Iliad, vii. to xii. . 1s. 6d.
7 HOMER. Iliad, xiii. to xviii. . 1s. 6d.
8 HOMER. Iliad, xix. to xxiv. . 1s. 6d.
9 HOMER. Odyssey, i. to vi. . 1s. 6d.
10 HOMER. Odyssey, vii. to xii. 1s. 6d.
11 HOMER. Odyssey, xiii. to xviii.
12 HOMER. Odyssey, xix. to xxiv.; and Hymns.
13 PLATO. Apology, Crito, and Phædo.
14 HERODOTUS, i. ii.
15 HERODOTUS, iii. to iv.
16 HERODOTUS, v. vi. and part of vii.
17 HERODOTUS. Remainder of vii. viii. and ix.
18 SOPHOCLES; Œdipus Rex. . 1s.
19 SOPHOCLES; Œdipus Coloneus.
20 SOPHOCLES; Antigona.
21 SOPHOCLES; Ajax.
22 SOPHOCLES; Philoctetes.

23 EURIPIDES; Hecuba.
24 EURIPIDES; Medea.
25 EURIPIDES; Hippolytus.
26 EURIPIDES; Alcestis.
27 EURIPIDES; Orestes.
28 EURIPIDES. Extracts from the remaining plays.
29 SOPHOCLES. Extracts from the remaining plays.
30 ÆSCHYLUS. Prometheus Vinctus.
31 ÆSCHYLUS. Persæ.
32 ÆSCHYLUS. Septem contra Thebas.
33 ÆSCHYLUS. Choëphoræ.
34 ÆSCHYLUS. Eumenides.
35 ÆSCHYLUS. Agamemnon.
36 ÆSCHYLUS. Supplices.
37 PLUTARCH. Select Lives.
38 ARISTOPHANES. Clouds.
39 ARISTOPHANES. Frogs.
40 ARISTOPHANES. Selections from the remaining Comedies.
41 THUCYDIDES, i. . . . . 1s.
42 THUCYDIDES, ii.
43 THEOCRITUS, Select Idyls.
44 PINDAR.
45 ISOCRATES.
46 HESIOD.

LONDON : JOHN WEALE, 59, HIGH HOLBORN.
WHOLESALE AGENTS, LOCKWOOD & CO., 7, STATIONERS' HALL COURT, E.C.